Whole-School Strategies for Anger Management:

Practical materials for senior managers, teachers and support staff

Teach to
Inspire

www.teachingexpertise.com/teachtoinspire

Whole-School Strategies for Anger Management:

Practical materials for senior managers, teachers and support staff

Michael Hymans

This book is commissioned by Barbara Maines and George Robinson for Teach to Inspire, a series for Optimus Education.

Author:

Michael Hymans

Designer:

Jess Wright

Editors:

George Robinson and Barbara Maines

Copy Editor:

Mel Maines

Printed by: Hobbs the Printers Ltd.

Registered Office: Brunel Road, Totton, Hampshire SO40 3WX

Registered Number: 422 132

Published by Optimus Education: a division of Optimus Professional Publishing Ltd.

Registered Office: 33-41 Dallington Street, London EC1V 0BB

Registered Number: 05791519

Telephone: 0845 450 6407 Fax: 0845 450 6410

www.teachingexpertise.com

ISBN 978-1-906517-20-5

A CD-ROM is attached to the inside front cover and is an integral part of this publication.

Contents

Use of the CD-ROM

Many Teach to Inspire publications include CD-ROMs to support the purchaser in the delivery of the training or teaching activities. These may include any of the following file formats:

- PDFs requiring Acrobat v.3.

- Microsoft Word files.

- Microsoft PowerPoint files.

- Video clips which can be played by Windows Media Player.

- If games are included the software required is provided on the CD-ROM.

All material on the accompanying CD-ROM can be printed by the purchaser/user of the book. This includes library copies. Some of this material is also printed in the book and can be photocopied but this will restrict it to the black and white/greyscale version when there might be a colour version on the CD-ROM.

The CD-ROM itself must not be reproduced or copied in its entirety for use by others without permission from the publisher.

All material on the CD-ROM is © Hymans 2009.

Symbol Key

 This symbol indicates a page that can be photocopied from the book or printed from the CD-ROM.

Introduction

There has been much discussion recently amongst educationalists and researchers concerning the relationship between two key government policies:

1. Raising standards.

2. Encouraging inclusion.

The question being, how can schools devote efforts to raising standards of the majority of their pupils while, at the same time, directing resources to pupils whose presence has the potential to disrupt the smooth running of the school? There is evidence that mainstream schools are becoming increasingly reluctant to accommodate such pupils (Ainscow et al., 1999) and that, once they have been placed in a special school, mainstream schools are reluctant to re-admit them (Farrell and Tsakalidou, 1999). The government in recognising this problem developed new guidance for schools giving them more power to exclude. However, there is concern that government policies on inclusion may not be working for pupils with emotional, social and behavioural difficulties (ESBD) in the context of increased pressure to raise standards of attainment through teaching and assessing the National Curriculum under a more stringent inspection system.

Children with ESBD are amongst the most difficult to teach. Their behaviour often requires particularly skilful and vigilant management. This places their teachers under considerable pressure as they strive to provide a worthwhile and coherent education that offers pupils with ESBD opportunities to make steady progress, comparable where possible with that of their peers in 'ordinary' schools (Her Majesty's Chief Inspector, 1999). Some of these pupils may have temporary needs, perhaps provoked by sudden traumas in the family, or they may have had a long history of serious disturbing or delinquent behaviour. Alongside them may be children with conditions such as Tourette's Syndrome, Asperger's Syndrome or other psychiatric disorders.

Against this background there has been growing interest in emotional education (McCarthy and Park, 1998) and emotional literacy (Orbach, 1999 and Sharp, 2001). Educational Psychology Services, in particular, have been promoting the issue with wide-ranging agendas that have included workshops on anger management for both teachers and pupils (Faupel et al., 1998) that have a predominantly cognitive-behavioural orientation and have been delivered as part of the Personal, Social and Health Education (PSHE) curriculum aimed at promoting pupils' spiritual, moral, cultural, mental and physical development at school and in the wider community. Understanding emotions such as anger is, of course, directly connected with motivation and with cognitive achievement. Dealing with anger, for example, helps young people to develop better relationships and a sense of psychological and mental wellbeing. Emotionally developed young people are better equipped to live with change. Educating the emotions leads to a more effective workforce because our moral outlook and value systems are deeply shaped by our attitudes and feelings. Our sense of meaning and purpose is derived as much from feeling as from understanding.

The Audit Commission's report, Special Educational Needs: A Mainstream Issue (2002), highlighted that children who should be able to be taught in mainstream settings are sometimes turned away, usually because too many staff feel ill-equipped to meet the wide range of pupil needs in today's classrooms. Families of such children also face unacceptable variations in the level of support available from their school, local authority or local health service.

National Statistics (Permanent and Fixed Term Exclusions from Schools and Exclusion Appeals in England, 2003/04) showed that there were 9,880 permanent exclusions from primary, secondary and all special schools in 2003/04, which represented 0.13% of the number of pupils in schools (13 pupils in every 10,000). Compared with the previous year the number of permanent exclusions had increased by 6%, although since 1997/98 the overall number of permanent exclusions had decreased by almost 20%.

Removing Barriers to Achievement (DfES, 2004) was aimed at supporting schools in developing effective inclusive practice through a new Inclusion Development Programme. However, it cannot be stated strongly enough that all schools should work hard at making pupils feel that they are part of the school community and that they have something to contribute. The concept of inclusion has moved on from meaning all pupils being included in mainstream schools to the much more helpful notion of all schools working together as part of an inclusive local authority. An inclusive school is likely to be an effective school and an effective school is certain to be inclusive.

The challenge to all teachers is to desist from assuming that children are the problem and that they can all be adapted to the demands of the curriculum. It is the curriculum which must be adapted to the needs of the children. In this context the government has taken steps within the national behaviour strategy (for example, the SEAL curriculum which encompasses social and emotional aspects of learning) to improve the quality of education for children with more severe ESBD. This timely publication can be used to complement and extend the DfES SEAL programme, especially into Key Stage 3 and will also have relevance for schools seeking to work with groups as part of the extended schools programme.

The SEAL curriculum is aimed at ensuring that all pupils, not just those with ESBD, have:

> …a universal entitlement for children to take part in carefully planned work that is based on evidence-based good practice in order to help them develop the social, emotional and behavioural skills needed to succeed.

Primary National Strategy (DfES, 2005)

The SEAL curriculum evolved out of the Primary National Strategy (DfES: Improving behaviour and attendance) and drew on the work of Hellaby (2004) and Goleman (1995). In Walking the Talk, Hellaby suggested that teachers should know that children must feel happy and secure within the school environment in order to learn successfully.

The Primary National Strategy (PNS) concluded that children who are anxious, angry or depressed don't learn and do not take in information efficiently or deal with it well. The PNS also makes reference to the work of Reva Klein, Chair of The International Consortium on School Disaffection, who promotes the need for children to learn how to communicate their feelings, set themselves goals and work towards them, interact successfully with others, resolve conflicts peaceably, control their anger and negotiate their way through the many complex relationships in their lives today and tomorrow.

The Children Act (2004), which secured Royal Assent on 15 November 2004, placed a duty on Local Authorities to improve children's wellbeing. Wellbeing is defined by reference to the Every Child Matters (ECM) five outcomes, that is:

1. Being healthy.

2. Staying safe.

3. Enjoying and achieving.

4. Making a positive contribution.

5. Economic wellbeing.

The Children Act also promoted early intervention and preventative work.

However, when commenting on the annual school exclusions statistics published on 26 June 2007, Schools Minister, Jim Knight, said the figures reflected the hard line schools were taking on discipline, adding that new powers introduced earlier this year would help to deliver further improvements in behaviour. The statistics showed that the number of permanent exclusions for very serious misbehaviour had fallen by 3% from 9,440 to 9,170 in all maintained primary, secondary and special schools, which adds up to a drop of 25% since 1997-98.

At the same time, the number of fixed period exclusions in secondary schools rose by 4% to 343,840 last year, suggesting that more schools are using short suspensions as a way of clamping down on lower level misdemeanors before they escalate to the point where permanent exclusion is necessary.

Other key findings from the statistics were that boys accounted for nearly four-fifths of all permanent exclusions, with pupils aged 12-14 years most likely to be excluded and that the most common reasons for permanent exclusions were persistent disruptive behaviour, physical assaults against another pupil and verbal abuse or threatening behaviour against an adult.

Jim Knight further commented:

> The rise in fixed period exclusions reflects the tough approach schools are taking to address bad behaviour. They are using the short, sharp shock of a suspension to nip problem behaviour in the bud, and this is helping to stop this escalating to the point where permanent exclusion becomes necessary.

> We want to build upon this hard line on discipline, which is why we have given schools tough new disciplinary powers to instill the "behavioural 3Rs" – rules, responsibilities and respect – more effectively. A teacher's authority must be absolute, and if young people do badly misbehave, we fully support schools taking the tough decision to exclude.

However, according to Gillean McCluskey (2005), although exclusions associated with overtly challenging behaviour was seen as a very serious process by nearly all the young people in her study (61 pupils aged 13-16 years), it was also found that most of these pupils, irrespective of direct involvement in the exclusion process, regarded exclusions as entirely ineffective or only partially effective and sometimes counter-productive. These findings were consistent across the four schools that the pupils attended: they applied to both males and females as well as to excluded pupils and those who were not excluded.

The study also found that most young people, whatever their relationship with school and regardless of school attended, were dissatisfied with their school discipline system. McCluskey concluded by saying:

> It should be of immediate concern to schools that exclusion, a central, long-established part of the school discipline process, is seen simultaneously as significant and yet ineffective. It seems likely that experience of this paradox must effect pupils' engagement with the broader priorities of schools in terms of discipline. There is therefore, a need for a measured re-appraisal of the aims and use of this sanction of last resort.

The rationale for this book stems from the earlier work of Educational Psychology Services' workshops on anger management and the important links with emotional literacy. The contrast between anger management and conflict resolution (Chapter 1) is used to describe anger as an emotion and to illustrate its effect on individuals and others. This is in contrast to conflict which arises largely out of disagreement and disharmony and is seen as an inevitable part of growing up. Chapter 1 also provides the reader with some possible strategies and interventions based on children's needs for both individual staff and for senior leadership teams.

As this book is predominantly aimed at senior leadership teams in schools, a whole-school approach to anger management is outlined (Chapter 2) and suggests that, when properly channelled, anger can be a positive and productive force for change. 'Ten Features of Success' are used as a useful checklist for schools considering drawing up a whole-school anger management strategy. A 4Rs framework for teaching positive behaviour is also adopted in Chapter 2 and Chapter 3 outlines the teacher skills necessary to implement this framework.

A cognitive behavioural approach is adopted throughout and this approach is used to describe anger in terms of a Firework Model and Storm Metaphor in Chapter 4. Visual imagery and relaxation techniques are defined in Chapter 5 as these are essential parts of any anger management programme. Guidance for how best to set up, run and evaluate groups is included in Chapter 6 and a ten-session anger management group work intervention is detailed in Chapter 7. Chapter 8 extends the use of the cognitive behavioural approach with individuals by demonstrating how behavioural contracts can be used. It illustrates the powerful use of Positive Psychology when working with individual children by focusing on being happy, setting meaningful goals, reframing negative thoughts, focusing on developing competencies and finding time for pleasant activities.

How to Use this Book

For each chapter there is a series of activities aimed at reinforcing the points made and to facilitate staff discussions in order to promote the possible review and/or revision of school development plans, behaviour policies, classroom rules and general approaches to anger management and prevention in school. These activities are either at the end of the chapter or contained within the main body in shaded boxes and, of course, Chapters 6 and 7 deal directly with anger management group interventions. At the end of each chapter there are some reflective questions and issues for consideration by the reader.

It is suggested that senior managers or leaders of pastoral support teams lead and facilitate the activities and draw up proposals for whole-school approaches and school policy development based on the outcomes from the activities.

Two PowerPoint presentations accompany the book. The first session can be delivered separately from the second session as a 90 minute twilight activity. Or the two sessions can be combined and delivered as a half-day INSET for staff. The purpose of the two sessions is to raise staff awareness of anger and conflict, for themselves as adults and for them to use their understanding to help children and young people.

The book contains activities and tasks that can be used for staff development work. These are contained within the shaded areas. If the reader is not working with a group these activities and tasks can be completed as self-reflective exercises.

Chapter 1: Anger Management Versus Conflict Resolution

What is Anger?

Anger is an instinctive feeling of extreme displeasure and it is a secondary emotion usually arising out of a primary emotion such as fear. It can lead to acrimony, animosity, annoyance, antagonism, exasperation, fury, hatred, irritation, outrage, resentment and violence. Dennis Stott (1974) links anger to hostility as one of a number of core syndromes of social adjustment difficulties. He defines hostility as follows:

> The child has lost faith in the loyalty of adults, usually because of expressions of rejection or actual rejection within the home and sets out to provoke a breach as a means of relief from her/his insecurity.

According to Stott, hostility can take two forms:

1. Provocative acts calculated to make the child an outcast.

2. A sullen avoidance of offers of friendship.

Of course anyone can be angry – that is easy, but to be angry with the right person, to the right degree, at the right time, for the right purpose, and in the right way is not easy. However, anger is an essential part of being human and is a potentially useful emotion, as identified by Daniel Goleman's (1995) work on emotional intelligence and the introduction of the SEAL curriculum. Getting in touch with our emotional intelligence can help us to understand our own anger and to understand children's anger. It highlights the importance of continually trying to manage our feelings effectively especially in the role of senior leaders, teachers, teaching assistants and other support workers.

There are four main reasons why people act in an aggressive manner:

1. Fear that something will be taken away from them or that they will lose something they consider important.

2. Frustration at not being able to communicate in any other way.

3. Intimidation or to bully another person into giving in.

4. Manipulation – using temper tantrums as a way to emotionally control other people and manipulate them.

What is Conflict?

Conflict is a state of open, prolonged fighting, disagreement and disharmony where the people involved fail to be in accordance with each other. Conflict may result in arguments, animosity, antagonism, confrontation and dispute, to name but a few of the synonyms in Rogers' Thesaurus.

It would seem logical that as children and young people gain skills and experience in working together they would be less likely to get involved in conflict with each other. However in reality the opposite is true. It is almost inevitable that on the road to maturity young people will go through a period of bickering with each other and will sometimes display inappropriate behaviour towards their teachers. This is because decisions previously arrived at by young people are suddenly no longer acceptable and they will polarise between teachers who are perceived as traditional and those who are perceived as more radical.

The length of this period of bickering will vary according to how it is handled and managed by teachers. By acknowledging conflict and dealing with it openly it is possible to resolve many problems and young people can then emerge with improved skills and attitudes.

The reasons for conflict are not always completely clear. However, where teachers have been successful in confronting problems, it is evident that conflict not normally expressed will begin to emerge. Another explanation is that young people's variation of divergent ideas and values will lead to conflict. Disagreements on definitions of objectives, differences about strategies for achieving them, interpersonal grievances and collisions of values and belief systems will all come to the surface. Young people may manufacture problems in order to test whether their teachers really welcome open confrontation of problems. The conflict can also result as an expression of rebellion against the teachers' leadership. If young people are successful at taking responsibility for their own work they may begin to challenge teachers' control over classroom activities.

Conflict can be viewed as a natural reaction to increased personal intimacy resulting from group development activities. Getting to know others well, whilst rewarding, can also be unnerving and young people may unconsciously generate conflict within the class in order to re-establish some distance. Being successful may also make some young people uncomfortable, especially if this does not fit with previous patterns of behaviour and so, as a relief from their anxiety, they may unconsciously create conflict within the class to prove that they are not successful after all.

A useful starting point for understanding what can cause conflict in the classroom is described below (based on the work of Cowan, D. et al. 1992):

- A competitive atmosphere arising out of an attitude of everyone for themselves; a lack of skill of working in groups; the need to win because losing results in a loss of self-esteem; a lack of trust in the teacher or peers; the use of competition at inappropriate times.

- An intolerant atmosphere arising from the formation of cliques and scapegoating; an intolerance of racial or cultural differences; a lack of peer support that often leads to loneliness and isolation; a resentment of accomplishments, possessions or personal qualities.

- Poor communication can also contribute to conflict when pupils do not know how to express their needs and wishes effectively; have no forum for expressing their emotions and needs or are afraid to do so, and when pupils cannot listen to others.

- Conflicts can escalate when pupils are out of touch with their feelings; they do not know of non-aggressive ways to express their anger and frustration; they suppress their emotions; they demonstrate a lack of self-control.

- Classroom conflicts may escalate when the pupils and teachers do not know how to respond 'creatively' to conflict. In the case of pupils this may be as a result of lack of maturity or their stage of moral development. Parents and peer groups may also reward violent and aggressive approaches to conflict and there are plenty of models of this kind of behaviour if only from the television and electronic games.

- Pupils may manufacture problems in order to test out whether their teacher really does welcome open confrontation of problems. The conflict can result as an expression of rebellion against the teacher's leadership. If pupils are successful at taking responsibility for their own work they may begin to challenge the teacher's control over classroom activities. Being successful may make some pupils uncomfortable because their success does not fit with previous behaviour patterns and so as a relief from their anxiety they may unconsciously create conflict within the class to prove that they are not successful after all.

- Teachers can create conflicts by misusing their power because of their influence over the previously named factors and can contribute to classroom conflict whenever they place irrational or impossibly high expectations on pupils; they manage their classes with a multitude of inflexible rules; they continually resort to the authoritarian use of power and they establish an atmosphere of fear and mistrust.

Conflict Resolution

Pupils who are not able to negotiate often resort to conflict and, although pupils can be in conflict with each other without being angry, solving conflicts can help prevent pupils from becoming angry in the first place. As part of a whole-school policy conflict resolution and anger management go hand in hand and so we need both.

To shift conflict you have to shift perceptions and this can be achieved through effective communication. Emotions play a big role in keeping the conflict going. Many people come to a situation ready to fight it out. The main emotions involved here are fear and anger. Sharing emotions can be as important as sharing perceptions (Bodine and Crawford, 1998). In order to successfully resolve a conflict, pupils need to feel heard, understood and empowered. Usually in conflict situations communications are poor and participants are high in suspicion. Pupils also need to feel worthwhile and that they are capable. The focus for them has to be letting go of mistakes and looking to the future (Albert, 2003). Pupils who learn conflict resolution skills develop social competencies of co-operation, empathy, creative problem-solving, social cognitive skills and relationship skills (Bodine and Crawford, 2003). Conflict resolution encompasses negotiation, mediation, peer mediation and collaborative problem-solving.

Bodine and Crawford (2003) suggest four underlying tenets of conflict resolution:

1. Conflict is natural.

2. Differences can be acknowledged and appreciated.

3. Conflict when viewed in a positive way can be seen as a solution-building opportunity.

4. When conflicting parties come together and build on each other's strengths to find solutions, there is a positive knock on effect where a nurturing climate is created and individual self-worth is valued.

The activity 'How Do You Respond to Conflict?' (page 21) provides staff with an opportunity to explore a range of responses to conflict. It enables staff to reflect on whether a preferred response is used and to discuss the efficacy of the response. For example, it may be that the 'problem-solving' approach is preferred over the 'no nonsense' approach. However, in certain circumstances it may be better to employ the 'no nonsense' approach rather than simply 'ignoring'. The difference and implications of using a 'compromising' approach in preference to a 'smoothing' approach is also likely to produce some lively discussion especially in terms of what each of these approaches might mean for staff and children. The activity gives senior leadership team members a chance to investigate the degree of consistency among staff in their responses to conflict and what this might mean for a whole-school approach to conflict resolution.

The work of Bodine and Crawford (2003) offers some helpful and practical suggestions for staff which link directly with this activity. These are:

- Explaining to pupils that conflict can be a positive force.

If staff believe that conflict is a positive force, as a problem to be solved, and convey this attitude to pupils then conflict is likely to be lessened or even prevented! This is because when staff discuss in detail with pupils their own views about conflict and help pupils to explore their thoughts and feelings too it should become apparent to pupils that conflict is not inherently bad but that it is how some people choose to respond that is harmful.

- Providing support and reassurance for pupils who feel anxious about open expressions of conflict.

To provide security for such pupils staff must avoid the impulse to abolish all limits in response to criticism from some pupils as with the 'no nonsense' approach. Increased desires for independence to abdicate responsibility (as in, 'You take over and see if you can do better,') is likely to throw many pupils into an emotional tailspin. Extracting and using positive elements of pupil criticism demonstrates that conflict can be constructive, as in the 'compromising' approach.

- Resisting a more authoritarian style.

The 'no nonsense' approach is synonymous with 'being authoritarian', although it is important to provide support for students by staying in control of the situation. However, staff should try to resist the temptation to panic and tighten up in response to pupil criticism as this may only heighten the conflict. In general, teachers should try to regard conflict as an inevitable part of their pupils' growth towards maturity and they should therefore acknowledge and accept conflict and help them to learn constructive ways of coping with it.

- Responding to the feelings underlying the pupils' words.

In conjunction with 'active listening' (that is, remaining focused on the speaker, summarising or restating their remarks from time to time) staff can let pupils confronting them know that they understand and accept the feelings that lie behind the pupils' actual words. For example, a useful response to an outburst might be, 'You seem to be angry with me,' 'Can you tell me a little more about what is annoying you?' Responding to feelings, perhaps by engaging in a 'compromising' approach is also a useful technique for pupils to utilise in their conflicts with peers. Staff can demonstrate this technique and let pupils practice role-playing situations and can encourage pupils to utilise the approach whenever conflicts arise.

- Providing visible classroom reminders about conflict resolution strategies.

Visible classroom reminders will usually be in the form of notices around the classroom and framed in positive language, for example:

- We must accept that people are entitled to have different opinions and beliefs and we cannot force someone to change these.

- We must behave assertively and not aggressively.

- We must consider the rights of others and have respect for authority.

- We must communicate our feelings and needs in a straightforward way.

The language used in the strategies above can be modified or shortened according to the age and level of understanding of the pupils.

While acknowledging how difficult it can be to resolve conflict in large groups, Faupel et al. (1998) give some advice for positive conflict resolution:

Wait until everyone is calm (up to 45 minutes after an incident) and use good communication skills that include 'I' messages and no blaming.

One of the easiest ways to defuse an interpersonal conflict is to avoid accusatory language. One way to do this is by using statements about yourself and your feelings (called 'I' messages because they start with 'I feel' or 'I felt'), instead of 'you' messages, which start with an accusation, such as, 'You did this (bad thing),' or 'You are (another bad thing).' In other words, if you say, 'I felt let down,' rather than, 'You broke your promise,' you will convey the same information, but you will do so in a way that is less likely to provoke a defensive or hostile reaction from your opponent.

'You' messages suggest blame and encourage the recipient to deny wrong-doing or to blame back. For example, if you say, 'You broke your promise,' the answer is likely to be, 'No, I didn't,' which sets you up for a lengthy argument, or, 'Well, you did, too,' which also continues the conflict. 'I' messages simply state a problem without blaming someone for it. This makes it easier for the other side to help solve the problem without having to admit that they were wrong. Remembering to use 'I' messages can be difficult, however, because many people are not used to talking about themselves or their feelings (and in some cultures, this would be highly inappropriate). In addition, when we are in a conflict there is a very strong tendency to blame many of one's problems on the other side. So stating the problem in terms of a 'you' message is much more natural, and is more consistent with one's view of the problem. But by making the effort to change one's language, one can also reframe the way one thinks about the conflict, increasing the likelihood that a resolution can be found.

The No Blame Approach is synonymous with The Support Group Method. The Support Group Method, developed by Barbara Maines and George Robinson, was published as a distance learning pack in 1992 and recently updated (2008 & 2009). The approach addresses bullying by forming a support group of 'bullies' and/or bystanders. Without apportioning blame, it uses a problem-solving approach, giving responsibility to the group to solve the problem and to report back at a subsequent review meeting. When bullying has been observed or reported then The Support Group Method offers a simple seven-step procedure which can be used by a teacher or other facilitator. The Support Group Method has been proven effective in a variety of establishments around the world. The No Blame Approach is a general problem-solving technique based on the notion that blaming tends to make people behave defensively whereas not blaming offers the possibility of problem-solving in most situations.

Try to get the pupil to see it from the other person's point of view and acknowledge your part in the problem in order to try to generate the solution together. All interactions involve other people and what other people do and think may well result in them having different viewpoints from us even in the same situation. In fact every time we think about a situation, others are likely to be doing some thinking for themselves only they will be doing it differently. For example, a salesperson trying to sell you a used sports car will probably tell you that the engine is very powerful, the bodywork is in excellent condition, the car suits you and is good value for money. Your viewpoint is to see how much petrol the car uses, whether the car has been in a crash, what the car feels like to drive and whether the seats are comfortable and how the price of the car compares to other sports cars. 'How Do You Respond to Conflict?' (page 21) illustrates how our view on responding to conflict may be part of the problem.

Conflict resolution training has the potential to positively affect academic learning by equipping students with interpersonal skills that support collaborative school environments that are conducive to achievement. Many of the social skills that enable successful teamwork (for example, presenting positions, listening attentively, communicating understanding, generating integrative solutions, and reaching mutual agreement on the best course of action) are the same skills that underlie constructive conflict resolution. Empirical evidence indicates that without training, many students may never learn such skills (Johnson & Johnson, 1996). One of the crucial skills required for effective conflict resolution training is problem-solving.

Problem-Solving:

This problem-solving activity involves a series of steps each of which could be used as an activity in itself and led by a facilitator in a single session or a series of sessions using 'Problem-solving Activity 1'.

Step 1. Identifying the problem.

The facilitator needs to find a way of getting everyone's, or a sample of views about the problem experienced by staff from within the group. Depending on the size of the whole group, staff could work individually, in pairs or in small groups of four to six. Examples of staff problems, such as: 'Maria always calls out in class', 'I always have to tell Kofi to start his work several times and even then I have to stand over him before he will pick up his pencil,' could then be recorded. The use of a computer and interactive whiteboard would be extremely helpful for saving the work produced. If possible the views expressed should be paraphrased.

The facilitator could then introduce the value of using 'I' messages by adopting a script along the following lines:

'The best way to communicate a problem is to use the assertive "I" message. "I have a problem when everyone comes late to class because…" Taking ownership of the problem as opposed to saying, "You are always coming late to class," in itself changes the communication. If you start by blaming the other person then the communication goes downhill rapidly. And so it is more preferable to explain why this is a problem and request a change.'

Step 2. Brainstorm possible solutions.

With staff working individually, in pairs or in small groups, the facilitator should ask staff to come with any ideas for solving a particular problem no matter how crazy they might seem or even if not everyone agrees. The facilitator should encourage as many responses as possible by reminding staff that sometimes even the craziest idea can be adapted to form part of the solution.

The ideas should be recorded on a computer or interactive whiteboard.

If the whole group generates solutions that are agreeable to all, then the facilitator should proceed to Step 4.

Step 3. Evaluate solutions.

Still working individually, in pairs or in small groups, the facilitator should ask staff to come up with a potential plan of action based on the list of solutions. To help the group, the facilitator can ask them to rate the solutions generated in Step 2, say using a scale of one to five, where 'one' does not seem particularly helpful or useful and 'five' seems very helpful or useful. The rated solutions can be recorded using the whiteboard facilities. The facilitator should encourage the group to use solutions with higher ratings or combine two solutions to come up with a plan. The facilitator should remind the group that their plans should also use solutions that describe alternative actions to the problem behaviour.

Step 4. Draw up an intervention plan.

Still working individually, in pairs or in small groups, the facilitator should ask staff to write an action plan that sets out who will do what, where and when, and what will happen if they forget or do not follow through the agreed actions. An example or examples of action plans can be recorded by the facilitator for a follow-up session as in Step 5.

Step 5. Evaluate the plan.

The facilitator will set a time for group members to re-evaluate their plans both informally through normal school procedures such as weekly or daily meetings with pupils, reminding them that they should include in the plan when the review will take place. A week is usually enough time to evaluate whether the plan is working or not. And more formally at a follow-up meeting with the staff group, one or more plans could be evaluated through whole-group discussion.

It is important for the facilitator to keep the re-evaluation of the plan positive and to remind staff that they should do likewise with their pupils with no blaming and no criticising and so on. The facilitator should encourage staff to take on board any comments and suggestions made throughout this process and reinforce staff by praising and rewarding their efforts to resolve the issues. Staff can be reminded to do likewise with their pupils.

This activity could alternatively be undertaken by considering 'Tanya's Problem' instead of generating problems from staff. The facilitator would ask the staff group to develop a plan for Tanya (see scenario below) using steps 1 to 4.

Tanya cannot control her cussing. She uses cuss words at home, in the classroom, in the playground and just about everywhere. She has received several fixed term exclusions from school and is close to being permanently excluded. Tanya is falling behind with her work.

Sometimes it is necessary to make several plans before we find one that will work. A successful plan will work when we become aware of our behaviour and decide to change it. We can choose an alternative behaviour for the behaviour causing the problem. An alternative behaviour is a choice and this will be part of your plan. For example, instead of shouting, the class teacher could fold her arms and stare at the class until she got the class' attention, ring a bell or count aloud from one to ten.

When making choices or taking action you may find that there are more alternatives than you first thought. In looking at situations, there may also be more possible explanations than you had first thought. For example, a crashed car is found in a ditch and the driver is dead, what could have happened? The following are a list of possible suggestions:

- The driver had a heart attack or fainted.
- The car had a puncture or engine failure.
- The driver was drunk.
- The driver had misjudged the bend in the road.
- The driver was attacked by a bee or a wasp and lost concentration.
- The driver fell asleep.
- The driver had been murdered and then placed in the crashed car.

Albert (2003) identified a five-step plan for conflict resolution similar to the problem-solving approach but with a greater emphasis on feelings ('Problem-solving Activity 2' page 24). This five-step plan could be used in conjunction with the previous problem-solving activity. The problem-solving technique listed here is best done one-to-one but can be done with a small group. It is used between teachers and pupils but students can also be taught to use the technique themselves in a similar way to the preceding activities.

1. State problem.

In objective terms in that the behaviour is what you can see and hear. Stay away from vague language like 'Michelle has an attitude' or 'Wayne is aggressive.'

2. State the need.

In stating what you need from a situation and asking the student to state his or her needs, a clearer understanding can be reached which helps to shift people who are entrenched in their own point of view.

3. Describe the feelings.

The logic behind dealing with the feelings is to get the emotions out of the way so that a rational conversation can happen.

4. Discuss solutions.

Brainstorming is used to come up with a plan.

5. Decide on a plan.

The steps for implementing the plan and a timeframe for reviewing the plan are decided. It is usually a good idea to agree the plan in writing.

Finding the Best Resolution

Sometimes asking people to think of the last time they were involved in a conflict situation and to recall the details and how it was resolved is a particularly useful starting point. Noting the strategies used and other significant points and looking for alternatives, facilitates helpful discussions. This is because for a good resolution all parts of the problem from all the different points of view are solved. When working with people who are in dispute with each other it helps to separate the initial solution statement from the real needs of the people. Often people already have the problem solved in their own mind so all they want to talk about is their solution and sometimes they do not even mention the need the solution is meant to satisfy. The activity 'Solution Versus Need' (page 25) explores this dilemma further.

In the second part of the activity the staff group could then be asked to answer the following questions, using 'Solution Versus Need Part II' (page 26):

- Why is it easier to talk about our solutions rather than our needs?

- What kinds of questions can you ask pupils, who are in dispute with their peers in order to express their real need?

- Why do you think conflict cools down when people in dispute hear about the needs of others?

- What have you learnt from this activity that will help you manage conflict in your classrooms and around the school?

The answers to these questions could be used for follow-up work with staff in small or whole-group discussion and staff could be asked to consider using bulletin boards with the theme of conflict resolution in their classrooms. Pupils could be asked to compose mottoes, for example:

- To compromise does not mean losing face.

- If you cannot stand the heat get out of the kitchen.

Problem-Solving and Conflict Resolution

Conflict can escalate if there is an increase in exposed emotions (such as anger and frustration); there is an increase in perceived threat; more people get involved and take sides. Therefore, it is possible to de-escalate conflict if attention is focused on the problem and not the participants, if there is a decrease in exposure to emotion and perceived threat, if children were friends prior to the conflict, and if children know how to make peace or they have someone available to help them do so. If we look at anger as a way to communicate, then the goal of intervention is to teach a more appropriate way to communicate. Problem-solving and conflict resolution can be taught as alternatives to acting out behaviour.

In any problem situation it is wise to begin with the use of reflective listening and non-blaming 'I' messages. Reflective listening helps you to develop your understanding of the young person and helps them to clarify their thoughts. It focuses on feelings and experiences not just on what the young person says. Reflective listening has its roots in the fields of counselling and psychotherapy, particularly in Carl Rogers' (1942) 'client-centered' therapy. This is not to say that adults in schools should become therapists, but rather that this one therapeutic skill can be very useful in many everyday school situations. Reflective listening is used in situations where you are trying to help the speaker deal with something. There are two major aspects of reflective listening – the 'listener orientation' and the 'reflective technique'.

1. Listening Orientation

In reflective listening, the listener adopts what Rogers called 'the therapist's hypothesis'. This is the belief that the capacity for self-insight, problem-solving, and growth resides primarily in the speaker. This means that the central questions for the listener are not, 'What can I do for this person?' or even 'How do I see this person?' but rather 'How does this person see themselves and their situation?'

In reflective listening, it is important not only that the listener has an orientation with the four qualities of empathy, acceptance, congruence and acceptance, but that the speaker feels that the listener has this orientation. Consequently, a good listener tries to understand how the other is experiencing the interaction and to shape their responses so that the other person understands where they are coming from. Furthermore, the listener must be prepared to deviate from the four principles if that's what the other person wants. For example, if the other person asks for an opinion, the listener should give it, rather than avoid it as implied by the principles of empathy and acceptance.

2. The Reflective Technique

A listener can implement the elements of listening orientation through a method known as reflection. In reflection, the listener tries to clarify and restate what the other person is saying. This can have a threefold advantage:

1. It can increase the listener's understanding of the other person.
2. It can help the other person to clarify their thoughts.
3. It can reassure the other person that someone is willing to attend to his or her point of view and wants to help.

Listening orientation and reflection are mutually reinforcing in that your intention should be to focus on who you are listening to, whether in a group or one-on-one, so as to understand what he or she is saying. As the listener, you should then be able to repeat back in your own words what they have said to their satisfaction. This does not mean you agree with, but rather understand, what they are saying.

Empathy, acceptance, congruence and concreteness contribute to the making of reflective responses. At the same time, reflective responses contribute to the development and perception of the listening orientation. Because the goal of the process is for the other person, rather than the listener, to take responsibility for the problem, reflective listening means responding to, rather than leading, the other. Responding means reacting from the other's frame of reference to what the other has said. In contrast, leading means directing the other person to talk about things the helper wants to see the other explore.

Using open questions (such as who? where? what? and when?) and reflective listening skills shows the student that you are listening and may help the student to clarify what they want, what you want and how it can be achieved. Closed questions close down communication. These include stating the obvious like, 'Do you think I can wait here all day?', 'Do you think I am stupid?' or comments like, 'That's too bad, well just get on with it,' or 'I don't want to hear it.' Nelsen et al., (2001) recommend that we 'stop telling and start asking'. Closed questions are those where the student can give a yes or no answer. Knowing when to keep quiet and listen is an important skill – do not rush to give a solution but allow the students to arrive at their own solutions. Often pupils tell us things at times when we are preoccupied or at times when we cannot give them the hearing they need. Feel free to put the student off at the time, but arrange an appropriate time when you can listen to them later. Simply say that what they are telling you is too important to rush and can you schedule a time to meet them and discuss it fully. Be sure to follow up on this. If they have come to you with a problem go back later and check that it has been sorted out or simply ask them how it is going.

In order to problem-solve children need certain skills. First, pupils have to be able to recognise that a problem exists. They may need help in identifying their feelings. They may have poor reasoning skills, weak logical or sequential thinking skills, or they may have poor memory. A difficulty in any of these areas will make it hard to implement problem-solving strategies. These difficulties must be remedied or a way to bypass them identified before proceeding. Children who have these basic skills can solve problems but we must have faith in them and their ability to work through and find solutions (Nelson et al., 2001).

Second, it is hard sometimes to trust that our students can make choices and decisions. This demands that we adopt the Adlerian position of driving from the back seat. The Adlerian position, as described in Ellenberger (1970), is based on the notion that young people are not typically aware of the convictions that drive their lives. The style of life is the blueprint or map for coping with experience but it nevertheless remains mostly out of one's awareness – Adler's process of understanding the unconscious. Thus both the construction of the individual's unique style of life and the goals and core convictions contained therein are also essentially unconscious.

At the core of Adler's integrated complex of philosophy, theory and practice was, according to amongst others, Russell (1951) and Ehrenwald (1991), a vigorously optimistic, humanistic view of life. Authors such as Russell and Ehrenwald suggest that Adler offered a value-oriented psychology which envisioned human beings as capable of profound co-operation in living together and striving for self-improvement, self-fulfillment and a contribution to the common good. Indeed, Adler predicted that if we did not learn to co-operate, we would run the risk of eventually annihilating each other.

Thus, if we were to distill his view of the human condition into one main idea, it would be the concept of the 'Social Human', inextricably interconnected with others and all of nature. The central problem that humans face is how to live on this planet together, appreciating what others have contributed in the past, and making life better for present and future generations.

Thirdly, in order to implement some of these ideas we have to trust and let go of some of our controlling ways in the process in the following ways:

- All parties must agree on the solution before it can become a plan and this is where we are able to give choices within limits.

- The teacher must set the limits on the behaviour.

- The teacher must structure what is acceptable in agreeing solutions.

- If the teacher is not open to trying the new suggestions (as long as they are reasonable), then the process will fail and the students will become discouraged.

Anger Management

Learning to control anger is a developmental skill. The frontal cortex, which is the part of the brain that controls the ability to inhibit impulses, takes 23 years to develop fully. From a developmental perspective younger children display no ability to control their anger and aggression. The typical two year old will act out all their anger. They have no ability to control their impulses – 'I want it and I want it now and if I can't have it I will fight for it'. Children at this stage will hit out, kick and bite. Gradually by the time they reach school age most children can control their impulses. By the end of primary school, children can delay their angry impulses and fight at times when there is no adult to prevent them, for example, pick a fight outside the gate of the school. The form of aggression is different, usually limited to punches confined to the upper body and ribs.

As we move into adolescence we need to remember the pressures and the behavioural imperatives of this transitional stage. At secondary level adolescents channel most of their aggressive impulses into games or competition; they either diffuse this destructive energy in sport themselves or by watching others compete. Peer pressure, the need to conform, and the search for identity may result in risk-taking and challenging behaviours. Fighting in this age group is usually gang related. However, there are exceptions where you will see a 12 year old behaving like 'a teenage toddler' – acting out all their aggressive impulses and having a temper tantrum. This is a child who has never learned how to control this impulse. This student has 'lost it' when you observe the tantrum. He is unable to hear anything you are saying and is unable to stop himself.

The way the pupil communicates and their body language is the key to identifying why they are acting in an angry or aggressive manner. They may look fearful, frustrated or threatening. Pupils who have never developed the skills to control their impulses and are emotionally stuck in the terrible twos usually act aggressively out of fear or frustration. Teachers can learn to recognise the early warning signs. These can include sudden changes in facial expression together with a lack or overuse of eye contact (such as 'cold' stares), sudden changes in body posture (slumping of shoulders or tensing of neck muscles), face reddening, sweating brow, talking quickly and excessively or suddenly 'going quiet'.

Seeing problem behaviour in a developmental context gives it different meaning and implies a different type of response. Teachers typically respond with a teaching solution to a learning error and a moralistic response to a behavioural error. In fact, behavioural mistakes are an inevitable part of learning how to behave and are developmental; what we need to do is place the emphasis on teaching student's new skills and guiding their behaviour in a positive direction. During a crisis reducing the perceived threat or helping the student to communicate can de-escalate the situation.

Pupils who use anger to intimidate a person present as very much in control, as calm yet frightening. They make their threats or demands in a controlled manner.

With these pupils the best thing to do is not to fight but not to give in. State the consequences of the behaviour if they follow out their threat and quote the school policy in this area. Sometimes instead of getting locked into a power battle giving a face-saving way out can help diffuse the situation.

Consider the following scenario: At the end of the first lesson and just before morning break Stefan accidentally bumped into Ahmed. You overhear Ahmed say to Stefan, 'What do you think you're doing messing with my girlfriend Tyrika? I'm gonna knife you real soon when you aint expecting it.' You decide to intervene and remind Ahmed of the consequences of such behaviour both for Stefan and Ahmed, making reference to the current situation with knife crime and how the school and society responds to identified perpetrators of such crimes. He tells you to butt out otherwise he will get his older brother's mates to sort you out too. You then suggest that maybe the two boys and Tyrika could use the school's peer mediation process to resolve this conflict, briefly explaining the rationale and possible outcomes.

Pupils who try to use anger to manipulate present as calm, yet they have an inconsistent pattern of demands. The topic of conversation changes and the pupil may describe other incidents where they felt hard done by and begin an entirely different conversation than the one you were having. There is a clear underlying thread in this exchange: you give me what I want and I won't lose control. In this situation the 'broken record technique' works well – simply stick to the original topic and state consequences of behaviour. It can also help to arrange a meeting at a later date to get all the concerned parties together so that all the facts are clear. When there is good communication it is difficult to manipulate a person or situation.

Consider this scenario – you notice Jermayne is picking on Emile in your English lesson and then you see that Anand intervenes and tries to stand up for his friend Emile. You become irritated because all three pupils are not working and what's more they are preventing others from working too. You then ask Anand to come to the front of the class so that you can talk to him on his own. He refuses and questions loudly in front of the whole class why you are picking on him. He then tells you of other occasions when he has been wrongly accused for disrupting your lessons. He says that he went home and told his mum about these other incidents and that she is going to make an appointment to see the headteacher.

You then suggest that you will write to Anand's mum to invite her into school for the three of you to meet to discuss Anand's concerns and that you may want to draw up some kind of agreement that incorporates expectations of behaviour with appropriate rewards for appropriate behaviour and consistent consequences for inappropriate behaviour: this agreement may be incorporated within a home-school book.

The angry child activity below explores the theme of the angry child and invites staff to consider the triggers to the child getting angry, to think through their actions and the resultant consequences.

Ask the group to very quickly jot down the answers to the questions below based on the last time they saw an angry child:

- What did you see?

- What did you do?

- How did you feel?

- How did it end?

A staff group discussion about the predominant and different actions could be used to explore the most effective whole-school approaches to the angry child. In this respect the facilitator would be looking which actions (2nd bullet point) led to successful outcomes (4th bullet point) and which actions were unsuccessful.

The questions for the staff group are:

- How can individual staff do more of what are successful actions?
- How can individual staff avoid actions that they know lead to unsuccessful outcomes?
- What role can the senior leadership team play in ensuring that staff actions lead to successful outcomes?

The discussion can also highlight that sometimes staff may see a child getting angry and sometimes they may not. It should provide staff, especially the less experienced ones, with some clues as to what they are likely to see when children get angry. It also gives permission for staff to express their feelings about managing difficult situations with angry children in a well-planned and safe activity.

Summary

Anger is an essential part of being human and is a potentially useful emotion and conflict can be viewed as a natural reaction to increased personal intimacy especially in group settings such as schools. Learning to control anger is a developmental skill and teachers can learn to recognise the early warning signs of children getting angry by the way in which pupils communicate and use their body language. Pupils who are not able to use skills of negotiation often resort to conflict. One of the easiest ways for teachers to defuse interpersonal conflict is to avoid accusatory language and to try to get pupils to see the other person's point of view. Sometimes asking pupils to think of the last time they resolved a conflict situation successfully is the means of finding the best resolution to a presenting problem: active listening and reflection are useful teacher tools.

Questions for You to Consider

- What conclusions might you draw from observations of people acting in an aggressive manner?
- How might you explain conflict in your classroom?
- What principles would you draw on to help resolve this conflict?
- What practical suggestions would you give to a colleague to help them better manage conflict in their classroom?

How Do You Respond to Conflict?

Read the statements below. If a statement describes a response you usually make to your classroom write '3' in the appropriate space. If it is a response that you occasionally make write '2' and if you rarely or never make the response write '1'.

When there is a classroom conflict, I:

1. Tell the pupils to pack it in.	
2. Try to make everyone feel at ease.	
3. Help the pupils to understand each other's point of view.	
4. Separate the pupils and keep them away from each other.	
5. Let the headteacher handle it.	
6. Decide who started it.	
7. Try to find out what the real problem is.	
8. Try to work out a compromise.	
9. Turn it into a joke.	
10. Tell them to stop making such a fuss over nothing.	
11. Make one pupil give in and apologise.	
12. Encourage the pupils to find alternative solutions.	
13. Help them to decide what they will give in on.	
14. Try to divert attention from the conflict.	
15. Let the pupils sort it out as long as nobody is hurt.	
16. Threaten to send the pupils to the headteacher.	
17. Present the pupils with some alternatives from which to choose.	
18. Help everyone feel comfortable.	
19. Get everyone busy doing something else.	
20. Tell the pupils to settle it in their own time after school.	

Chapter 1

How Do You Respond to Conflict? (Cont)

Scoring: Enter the appropriate numbers for each of the above questions in the columns below and then add the totals for each column.

I		II		III		IV		V	
Question	score	Question	score	Question	score	Question	score	Question	score
1		2		3		4		5	
6		7		8		9		10	
11		12		13		14		15	
16		17		18		19		20	
TOTAL		TOTAL		TOTAL		TOTAL		TOTAL	

In which column did you score the highest?

I = the no-nonsense approach.

II = the problem-solving approach.

III = the compromising approach.

IV = the smoothing approach.

V = the ignoring approach.

Use a group discussion about what the predominant and different approaches might mean for a whole-school approach to conflict resolution.

Problem-Solving Activity 1

Step 1. Identify the problem.

Step 2. Brainstorm possible solutions.

Step 3. Evaluate the possible solutions.

Step 4. Draw up an intervention plan.

Step 5. Evaluate the plan.

Problem-Solving Activity 2

Step 1. State the problem.

Step 2. State the need.

Step 3. Describe the feelings.

Step 4. Discuss the solutions.

Step 5. Decide on a plan.

Solution Versus Needs – Part I

When working with people who are in dispute with each other it helps to separate the initial solution from the real needs of the people. Often people already have the problem solved in their own minds so all they want to talk about is their solution and sometimes they do not even mention the need the solution is meant to satisfy.

For example:

Solution Statement

Need Statement

Stop all this talking and laughing.

I need peace and quiet so that I can concentrate.

List examples from staff based on classroom experiences:

Solution Statements

Need Statements

Solution Versus Needs – Part II

Why is it easier to talk about our solutions rather than our needs?

What kinds of questions can you ask pupils in dispute with their peers to get them to express their real needs?

Why do you think conflict cools down when people in dispute hear about the needs of others?

What have you learnt from this activity that will help you manage conflict in your classrooms and around school?

Chapter 2: A Whole-School Approach to Anger Management

Anger is a very powerful emotion, which when properly channelled can be a positive and productive force for change. When this does not happen, anger can be destructive leading to aggressive outbursts which are likely to be distressing for those directly involved, as well as for those who witness the aggression.

It is important for school staff to have an understanding of anger, how it is expressed and ways of managing their own and others' anger. There is a high probability that during their careers staff will encounter instances of aggressive behaviour in a school setting. These instances could cover a number of permutations including pupil to staff, pupil to pupil, staff to pupil, staff to staff, parent to staff and staff to parent. The aggressive behaviours could range from relatively minor instances of verbal abuse to serious physical assault. It is important to stress that serious incidents of aggressive behaviour are comparatively rare and that minor incidents are far more common but that cumulatively, these minor incidents can result in high levels of stress for school staff.

The development of an anger management strategy in a school should be considered as part of a whole-school approach to managing behaviour. In a typical school community there is a need on the one hand to discourage problematic and disruptive behaviour through the use of appropriate sanctions. On the other hand, there is a need to notice, acknowledge and reward appropriate behaviour. A whole-school approach to behaviour management should balance the need to manage behaviour with training in self-discipline. A positively proactive whole-school management system moves beyond traditional punitive approaches by providing children with opportunities for learning self-discipline. From a preventative standpoint, all schools can benefit from a clearly defined and consistently applied behaviour management system that is designed to support pupils in managing their own behaviour.

With regard to the issue of violence, all of us must have been horrified by the media reports of violence in schools. Our children are exposed to increasing levels of violence and the psychological effects of such experiences on children are well known. Violent children usually come from violent homes where parents model violence as a means of resolving conflict and handling stress. Children who witness violence can display a gamut of emotional and behavioural problems, including low self-esteem, withdrawal, depression, self-blame, and aggression towards peers, family members, the wider community and property (Peled, Jaffe and Edelson, 1995). Massey (1998) refers to research studies which show that persistent exposure to violence adversely affects children's ability to learn. It is known that children who achieve in school and develop skills such as critical thinking, communication and problem-solving are better able to cope with stressful and perhaps even dangerous real life situations (National Commission for Education, 1996).

Hellaby (2004) has been quoted by the Government launch of the SEAL Curriculum in 2005 as follows, 'As every teacher knows, in order to learn successfully, children must feel happy and secure within the school environment.' In September 2009 senco-week@senco.teachingexpertise.com offered subscribers to SENCO Update ready-to-use assemblies to support schools in delivering SEAL in both primary and secondary schools. The ready-made SEAL assemblies are divided into 'themes' under the same headings as those used by the primary school SEAL programme namely:

- New beginnings.
- Getting on and falling out.

- Say no to bullying.
- Going for goals.
- Good to be me.
- Relationships and changes.

The assembly material for secondary schools is classified into five sections in line with the secondary school SEAL programme and these are:

1. Empathy.
2. Managing feelings.
3. Motivation.
4. Self-awareness.
5. Social skills.

The content of the assemblies material clearly highlights the importance of early intervention to help children develop the necessary thinking, communicative and empathetic skills in order to equip them to better manage aggression, conflict and confrontation. School staff, through the assemblies and in their classrooms, can model appropriate ways of managing problems, conflict, anger and stress: they can teach children that feelings are normal, including feelings of anger and hurt, but that violence is an unacceptable way of expressing anger, frustration and any other negative feelings. Staff can help children to learn how to manage their emotions without resorting to violence and they can teach children ways of avoiding becoming victims of violent acts through an emphasis on personal safety. This can and should be part of a whole-school programme.

Fitzsimmons (1998) identified four common features of whole-school behaviour management systems:

1. Total staff commitment to managing behaviour.
2. Clearly defined and well communicated sets of expectations and rules, where the consequences for not sticking to these are explicit with clear procedures for correcting rule breaking.
3. An instructional component for teaching pupils self-control and strategies for social interactions.
4. A support plan to address the needs of pupils with persistently challenging behaviour.

There is considerable similarity between Fitzsimmons' features and the four main components of a positive behaviour management programme:

1. Whole-school environment.
2. Rewards and sanctions.
3. Teaching of new behaviours.
4. Approaches to handling crises.

(Faupel, et al., 1998)

Faupel et al. (1998) comment that:

> Very few behaviour policies drawn up by schools currently address the issue of anger, and many simply expect children to conform and have no explicit strategies for either reacting effectively, or better still, teaching children how they might better manage their anger at school.

The steps in policy development are outlined by Faupel et al., as follows:

1. Establish a need for an anger management strategy.

This is likely to emerge from the school development plan and perhaps from monitoring of behaviour across the school which might include, for example, the number of children sent out of class or to the headteacher, children excluded from school for losing their temper, fighting. Feedback on children's behaviour will also happen as a result of comments made by visitors to the school, such as Ofsted, School Improvement Advisers, Educational Psychologists.

2. Establish staff commitment for a policy. Staff training may form part of this process.

The willingness or desire of staff to further their skills in the area of behaviour and classroom management, say via their performance management appraisals and discussions with senior leadership team staff following classroom observations, is evidence of staff commitment for a whole-school policy on behaviour management that will include anger management.

3. Prioritise and incorporate an anger management strategy with the school development plan with an associated action plan with time scales, targets and identified staff.

The outcomes from steps 1 and 2 above are likely to highlight the need for prioritisation for a whole-school anger management strategy to be incorporated within the school development plan. And, of course, all good school development plans will include associated action plans with objectives, targets, time scales and the necessary personnel to lead on the completion of the plan.

4. Practices that have a sound research base and/or proven record of success.

The cognitive behavioural therapy (CBT) approach, as described later, forms the underpinnings of the firework model and storm metaphor together with visual imagery and relaxation, and has a proven record of success in anger management group interventions with children and young people, as well as with individual interventions such as behaviour contracts. Personal Construct Psychology (PCP), which is another cognitive approach within a social context (that is the school), has a sound research base and a proven record of success. Whereas Positive Psychology (similar in approach to PCP), is just beginning to come into favour as a potential successful tool for anger management.

5. Consider preventative approaches as well as interventions and guidelines for tackling instances of aggressive behaviour.

Positive Psychology suggests that positive emotions (for example, happiness, interest, anticipation) broaden one's awareness and encourage novel, varied, and exploratory thoughts and actions. Over time, this broadened behavioural repertoire builds skills and resources. For example, a child's pleasant interactions with teachers can become a supportive relationship for that child. This is in contrast to negative emotions, which prompt narrow survival-oriented behaviours. For example, the negative emotion of anxious aggression leads to the specific fight-or-flight response for immediate survival.

And, of course, some of the skills that are explicitly targeted through the SEAL curriculum are:

- Be effective and successful learners.
- Make and sustain friendships.
- Deal with and resolve conflict effectively and fairly.
- Solve problems with others or by themselves.
- Manage strong feelings such as frustration, anger and anxiety.
- Recover from setbacks and persist in the face of difficulties.
- Work and play co-operatively.
- Understand and value the differences between people, respecting the right of others to have beliefs and values different from their own.

6. Incorporate arrangements to monitor, evaluate and review procedures and practices in preparation for any modification or abandonment of ineffective procedures.

The detailed account of implementing behaviour contracts is illustrative of the importance of incorporating arrangements for monitoring, evaluating and reviewing practices in preparation for any modification or abandonment of ineffective targets, rewards or sanctions.

A useful checklist for schools considering drawing up a whole-school anger management strategy is the 'Ten Features of Success', highlighted in the 1998 Faupel, et al. study. A summarised version of these features is described as follows:

1. Strong leadership by the headteacher in identifying anger management as a priority component of a behaviour policy.
2. A good atmosphere from shared values and attractive environment including, for example, values concerning anger management.
3. High expectations of pupils in terms of effective anger management.
4. A clear focus on teaching and learning of anger management strategies for staff and pupils to use.
5. Good assessment of pupils.
6. Pupils sharing responsibility for learning to manage their anger.
7. Pupils participating in the life of the school.
8. Incentives for pupils to succeed.
9. Parental involvement.
10. Extra-curricular activities to broaden pupil interests and build good relationships in school.

1. Strong Leadership by the Headteacher in Identifying Anger Management as a Priority Component of a Behaviour Policy

From DfES research (reported in Earley et al., 2002), 'outstanding headteachers' worked consciously and without exception towards the development of a senior management or leadership team that was seen as strong and effective by the rest of the staff in terms of consulting, being respectful and listening. They managed to be separate enough to lead the school, but be accessible enough to know how the school community wanted to be led. In the context of identifying anger management as a priority component of a behaviour policy, a member of the senior leadership team may wish to promote a focus and emphasis on seeing the behaviour plan as a positive solution through the use of the 'Empathy Exercise'.

The facilitator would ask participants to sit comfortably and relax with their eyes closed or gaze lowered and to practice '4:4 breathing' (that is, breathing in for the count of four and then out for four) and would then read the following empathy exercise slowly, pausing for participants to build up their images and answer your questions in their heads.

'Be comfortable in your seat. Close your eyes or lower your gaze. Notice your breathing. Relax.

Imagine you are a pupil right now in your own classroom. Where are you? Are you standing or sitting? Who is with you? What is on the wall next to you? What are you doing? Do you know if your teacher likes the kids in this class? How do you know? What expression does the teacher have on his face?

You might have some problems with the work you have been given. How do you feel? What will you do? Do you sometimes get into trouble? What do you sometimes do? What happens when you are in trouble? What does the teacher do? How does this make you feel? What happens next? What are the good things you do? How are your efforts recognised? How do you feel at the end of the day? What do you say about school to your family? How will you feel about school tomorrow?'

The facilitator will now need to bring the participants back to the present and this can be done by simply saying, 'When I count backwards from five you will slowly open your eyes or raise your gaze and come back into the present. Five… four… three… two… one.'

The facilitator would ask the participants to reflect on this experience privately for a few minutes and would then ask them to discuss with a partner how it felt to do the activity.

For staff to be able to examine and challenge their own as well as other colleagues practice, it is important for them to discuss why it appears that some staff seem to have a better control of classes than others. These are some reasons that are often given and you may wish to add to the list:

- Effective and engaging teaching or support for pupils.

- Experience.

- Personality.

- Charisma.
- Status.
- Fear.

However, when discussing a variety of reasons it is important to focus on staff skills that can be learned; can staff learn to be charismatic?

You could as a facilitator ask staff, in small groups of six to eight, to consider the question of why it appears that some staff are better at helping pupils control their anger and manage their feelings than others and record their responses on flipchart paper. You could then ask participants to review as a whole group the staff skills that are most effective in creating a calm and purposeful classroom from the list generated from the small groups together with the list below of effective staff skills:

- Giving clear, concise and coherent instructions.
- Speaking clearly, quietly and confidently.
- Using humour to help pupils feel relaxed.
- Avoiding humiliation, sarcasm and put downs.

2. A Good Atmosphere from Shared Values and Attractive Environment Including, for example, Values Concerning Anger Management

Good relationships have a critical impact on anger management. The whole school community has an entitlement and responsibility to contribute to the development of others within the school community. A school ethos built on shared values, principles and beliefs is likely to enable positive relationships to flourish and it is through positive relationships that pupils will:

- develop self-confidence in their ability to express and manage their feelings
- feel supported when faced with a challenge and therefore feel less inclined to lose their temper
- gain trust and feel safe through such support.

Pupil-Staff Relationships

A facilitator might want to invite participants to choose a partner and think back to a time when they both were pupils at school. He would ask them to remember a teacher who made them feel 'bad' or who criticised them. Participants would then be invited to describe this incident to their partner. The facilitator would explain that the incident will not be discussed with the group.

After both partners have had the opportunity to share their experiences, the facilitator would invite the group to provide examples of the feelings generated by the incident which would then be recorded on the left hand side of a flipchart sheet. The range of feelings described would be discussed and the facilitator would ask for a brief discussion on the participant's emotional vocabulary recorded on the flipchart.

The facilitator would write the word 'Behaviour' on the opposite side of the flipchart and invite participants to suggest the behaviour we might expect to see as a result of the feelings described. He may wish to ask the following questions to stimulate the discussion:

- How did you react to future requests/instructions?
- How did it affect the effort you put into learning and behaving properly?
- How did your peers respond?

The facilitator would record these behaviours on the flipchart and would encourage participants to be specific in their descriptions of the behaviour they might see.

Feelings	Behaviour
Angry	Withdrawn
Upset	Crying
Sad	Sulking
Humiliated	Refusal to work
Embarrassed	Running away

The discussion that follows should elicit the following key points for the facilitator:

- Feelings affect and produce behaviours.
- Teachers are powerful and significant adults in pupils' lives. We are successful adults and yet we carry with us powerful feelings developed in our childhood.
- Feelings and behaviours affect and influence our ability to reach our full potential.

3. High Expectations of Pupils in Terms of Effective Anger Management

'No blame cultures' and ongoing dialogues about the school's aims and processes were common characteristics of outstanding headteachers in the DfES research (cited by Earley et al., 2002). This refers to headteachers having the courage to tackle staff and pupils who were underperforming in terms of effective anger management and having the vision to offer support for improvement. The focus on high standards of achievement, both academically and socially must be obvious in schools, with staff providing reminders of what is expected and celebrating the achievement of all, say through certificates and announcements at assemblies.

4. A Clear Focus on Teaching and Learning of Anger Management Strategies

Faupel et al. (1998) noted that, as with the management of behaviour, there are three levels at which children's anger management may be considered and these are at the:

1. Whole-school level.

2. Classroom or group level (Chapters 5 and 6).

3. Individual pupil level (Chapter 7).

At the whole-school level a number of steps have been identified as contributing to the formation of a well-developed policy that would impact positively at all three levels.

The 4Rs Framework for Teaching Positive Behaviour (from the National Behaviour Training Curriculum, Pilot, DfES 2004) Including Anger Management

This framework provides a structure that enables pupils to explore the fairness of positive behaviour management approaches and to take responsibility for their own choices. It is in fact the basis of any classroom behaviour plan in that it provides a consistent framework that can be taught to pupils by explaining the connections between the parts. It comprises an educational process that can be considered as fair and reasonable, reducing conflict and tension and allowing for choice and the development of skills.

The most appropriate time to introduce the framework to pupils is at the start of an academic year. The 4Rs framework should be the focus of at least the first lesson that each teacher presents to each class. Whole-class or small group discussion, together with Circle Time and drama or role-play activities, are appropriate teaching methods.

The 4Rs framework is represented diagrammatically as follows:

The 4Rs Framework

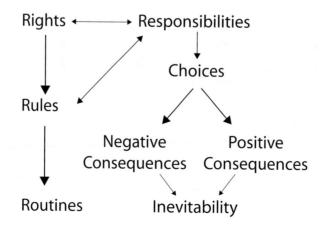

'Rights and responsibilities' are inextricably linked in that they are the basis on which classroom relationships, teaching and learning are built. They give the structural framework against which responsibility and accountability can be measured and are the expectations of the way things should be. Rights will be enshrined in the school's core values and principles and the beliefs that pupils and staff hold about rights and responsibilities must be congruent with these values and principles. Responsibilities correspond to rights and will be general and more specific.

5. Good Assessment of Pupils' Anger Management

Good assessment of pupil's anger management is likely to be by way of observations, and whole-school systems can include a number of different observation schedules and checklists. There is an example of a checklist (adapted from Ayers, Clarke and Ross, 1996) at the end of the chapter where 'personal and social development' and behaviour are rated. Such data can also be used as an initial baseline measure before any interventions are used. Similar baseline measures are used for implementing running anger management groups in Chapter 6.

The ABC Form of Behaviour

Once observations have been made it is often helpful to look at the accumulated information in a more analytical way. The ABC sheet enables teachers to collect and organise information in a way that reveals patterns of 'angry' behaviour in relation to three areas:

1. Antecedents:	The setting in which the 'angry' behaviour occurs including the event or events which happened immediately before the behaviour.
2. Behaviour:	The 'angry' behaviour itself in very clear and precise terms.
3. Consequences:	What happens afterwards and/or what seems to reinforce the 'angry' behaviour.

What is important about this sheet is the principle that 'angry' behaviour is related to a context, and that it is only when teachers can be precise and clear about what is happening that they can actually change the pattern through some kind of intervention. Both pupils and teachers tend to behave differently in different settings and equally they are influenced by what happens immediately or sometime before their current behaviour. The angry behaviour of a pupil can also be influenced by what they consciously or subconsciously think is going to happen. Through being precise about the angry behaviour itself it is possible to be clearer about what exactly needs to be changed.

It is important to remember that angry behaviour is likely to be repeated if the consequences of that behaviour are experienced as rewarding by the pupil. It is also important to remember that pupils can experience some so-called 'punishments' as rewarding. For example, being kept in at playtime (particularly on a cold day), for fighting in class may be experienced by the pupil as exceedingly rewarding!

The following table illustrates the basic version of an ABC sheet for use in observing pupils. It can be used by class/subject teachers or by an observer. If the behaviours causing concern (for example, fighting in class) are fairly infrequent, then the class teacher is likely to be the best person. The particular behaviour (for example, fighting) is recorded along with the date and time.

The ABC of Behaviour

Date and Time	Antecedents	Behaviour	Consequences
	Where does the (angry) behaviour occur? (For example, in the classroom or playground.) During what kind of task or activity does the behaviour occur? (For example, during a game of football.)	What did you actually see happen? (For example, David punched Jinesh.)	What happens after the behaviour has occurred? (For example, Jinesh started crying.) What does the pupil achieve from the angry behaviour? (Jinesh is out of the football game) How do staff react? (For example, listen to each child's account of the event.)

If time allows, brief details about contributing factors or contexts as well as outcomes of the angry behaviour can also be noted. Outcomes can include what happens to the pupil, how other pupils react and how staff react.

Antecedents	Behaviour	Consequences
How do you think the pupil(s) was (were) feeling before the incident? (For example, David was feeling that he would be excited by scoring a goal.)	Observable and objective description of the angry behaviour. (For example, David punched Jaynesh several times in the face and made his nose bleed after being tackled.)	How do other pupils react? What do they do/say? (For example, other pupils avoid tackling David and say that he is a bully.)
How do you think the pupils perceived the situation? (For example, David thought that Jaynesh had tackled him unfairly and had tried to hurt him.)		How do the pupils feel? (For example, Jaynesh felt sad and unhappy; David felt powerful.)

6. Pupils Sharing Responsibility for Learning to Manage their Anger

In general, personalised educational programmes that target key priorities for pupils as individuals are the means to make the most of their learning styles and realise their true potential and this approach can easily be applied to helping pupils manage their anger, say through the use of a behavioural contract described in Chapter 8. This approach demonstrates that the planning and evaluation of learning outcomes must take account of what matters to pupils. We must therefore seek to help pupils share responsibility for learning by presenting contract (performance) targets in forms that are useful for both parties (for example, 'child friendly' pictures or symbols as well as professional language), and by sharing and reviewing learning outcomes for the duration of the contract with pupils and staff and sometimes their parents and carers.

7. Pupils Participating in the Life of the School

Pupil participation is part of the inclusion Agenda and the Government's commitment to 'learning to listen' to ALL children and young people. In the DfES 'Working Together Giving Children and Young People a Say' (2004), pupil participation is defined as adults working with children and young people to develop ways of making sure that their views are heard and valued, as well as encouraging them to become more active partners in their education, including evaluation of their own learning. Listening to pupils views about their education leads to a better understanding of more appropriate and effective processes and provision. Research into effective schools shows that when pupils have an active role in the life of the school, and when they are given a shared responsibility for their own learning, the self-esteem of pupils is raised considerably. Schools should be warm, welcoming and open in order to make a difference as to how school is experienced by all pupils.

Every effort should be made to enable access for all pupils to activities that make up the whole life of the school, both formal and informal, inside and out of school hours and within their local communities Pupil participation can raise challenging questions around the balance of power in schools. Schools should start from a realistic point and then develop pupil participation in small stages as their collective confidence, trust and skills increase. Schools undertaking this journey should work towards a culture where children share power and responsibility for decision-making. This, coupled with an understanding of their right to be involved in all aspects of school life, should allow pupils to be effectively involved in school. The ethos, organisation and culture of a school should encourage and support pupil participation. Activities such as Circle Time can help pupils, even very young pupils, to feel valued and comfortable in expressing their views. School and class councils can also enable pupils to have their voices heard and to take part in group decision-making processes in a constructive way.

Getting started on the journey of participation requires careful planning, as well as a willingness to challenge existing norms and values and to take meaningful risks. Partnership is a vital element, enabling children, young people and adults to work things out together and discuss differences, even if it means disagreeing occasionally. This process also provides excellent opportunities to build respect for each other.

8. Incentives for Pupils to Succeed

In school we are frequently faced with challenges in the form of reluctant or disruptive learners who may take out their frustration in the form of angry challenges. It is perhaps worth asking your staff a question, 'What is the payoff from the pupils' perspective for engaging in the content of your lesson?' In planning a lesson, you may wish to consider whether, within your learning objectives, you have created 'a need' for the student. That 'need' in itself can then become an incentive. If the student can see the value in a lesson, he will be more motivated and less likely to create conflict.

You may then ask staff to consider the style in which they deliver their teaching. On a subconscious level, their tone of voice and body language will emit very powerful messages in terms of motivating students. Many teachers have now actively adopted a policy of non-verbal praise in the form of giving a thumbs-up sign, or simply consciously smiling at a pupil they wish to reward. This type of non-verbal encouragement, coupled with genuine verbal praise can go a long way towards enhancing self-esteem, something which is often sadly lacking in the low achiever or student who has problems managing his anger when he cannot learn or when things go wrong in small group work. It is frequently the most disruptive pupils who rarely receive any praise due to their poor behaviour and they are caught in a loop of disruption and admonition. In these situations it may be a case initially of praising such a pupil for what they are not doing, rather than for anything they are achieving. For example, just saying a 'well done for managing not to shout out' at the end of the lesson may encourage a child to behave better next time too. You could consider some creativity around the general reward scheme used within your school (for example, merit certificates, stickers or earning 'Golden Time').

The drawback of some of these systems is that it is usually the more able and well behaved who manage to gain such rewards. The introduction of school incentives gives you greater flexibility to encourage pupils of all abilities. Rewards need to given for genuine effort or achievements, however small. There can be a fine line between an incentive and a bribe. If the reward comes too easily, it will lose impact and staff will be seen as 'a soft touch.' It can sometimes be difficult for disruptive and angry pupils to receive praise in front of their peers since it can undermine their 'macho' image, so judge for yourself the best setting for giving out praise or rewards.

9. Parental Involvement

One of the ways that parental involvement influences achievement is through helping the child develop a pro-social, pro-learning self-concept (Desforges, 2003). It is not surprising therefore that parental involvement is associated with healthy adjustment (as say with anger management), as well as academic achievement. This is evident from pre-school days, where a positive home learning environment has been found to be associated with higher levels of co-operation, sociability and confidence, and lower levels of anti-social and worried or upset behaviour (Melhuish et al. 2001). Its impact is also evident among older children. For example, family support and the quality of the parent-child relationship predicted school adjustment in a sample of 10-12 year olds (Desforges, 2003). The positive impact of parental involvement remains even after controlling for the deleterious effects of social class, material deprivation and other forms of disadvantage. Indeed, Schoon and Parsons (2002) found that parental involvement helped to explain why some children experiencing multiple disadvantages were able to succeed despite their unpromising circumstances. At the other end of the spectrum, truancy is associated with low parental interest as well as poor relationships between parent, child and school (Graham and Bowling, 1995). Schools were obliged to introduce home-school agreements following the 1998 Schools Standards and Framework Act. A recent evaluation shows that take-up has been reasonable, but by no means universal (Coldwell et al. 2003). 75% of parents in around three quarters of schools in the research had signed an agreement but parents' the awareness of agreements is not strong. 35% of parents in a recent survey did not recognise the term home-school agreement (Williams et al. 2002).

Coldwell and colleagues (2003) conclude that agreements are only likely to be successful as part of a wider programme of parental involvement. Others question whether they are necessary at all and suggest the purpose of increasing parent-school co-operation would be better achieved by encouraging and enabling schools to develop home-school policies in genuine collaboration with parents and pupils. Indeed, although pupils are encouraged to sign agreements if they are deemed to understand their relevance, they are not formal partners. Neither is there any burden on schools to consult with pupils about their introduction. Rather, the onus of the relationship is between schools and parents, with the expectation that parents can ensure their children comply with the demands of the agreement – clearly an unrealistic expectation for some families.

10. Extra-Curricular Activities to Broaden Pupil Interests and Build Good Relationships in School

A recent study of extended schools concluded that they can make a positive impact on pupil attainment, attendance and behaviour by increasing engagement and motivation (Wilkin et al. 2003). However, it is early days to tell whether these approaches can really make a difference. Most initiatives are individualised and school specific, and the programmes have not been evaluated in ways that permit observers to draw clear conclusions about costs and benefits. Moreover, in their study of schools and area regeneration, Crowther et al. (2003) concluded that schools can have small-scale or localised effects, but there is no evidence that schools have larger effects that transform pupils' prospects or the communities in which they live.

An important issue in the development of extended schools is the impact of extra-curricular activities and support. These facilities cannot, of course, completely make up for a lack of parental interest. However, they do have the potential to make up some of the deficit in home support by offering an alternative resource in the school environment.

Summary

This chapter has suggested that the development of an anger management strategy should be considered as part of a whole-school approach to managing behaviour and that staff commitment for such a policy as well as staff training will need to be part of the process. Preventative approaches are strongly recommended and the 4Rs framework has been emphasised as an approach that enables pupils to explore the fairness of positive behaviour management in which classroom behaviour plans play a key role. A checklist for drawing up the whole-school anger management strategy is outlined on pages 30-40.

Questions for You to Consider

- How has your school raised staff awareness of the powerful influences of anger within the school community?

- How might your school make use of the SEAL curriculum as part of a preventative measure for anger management across the whole school?

- How does the 4Rs framework link with your whole-school behaviour policy?

- How does your school engender positive pupil-staff relationships?

An Anger Management Checklist for Staff

Name of Pupil:

Please put a tick (√) in the box for each statement under each of the headings.

1. Personal and social development	1	2	3	4	5
	Hardly ever	Sometimes	About half the time	Much of the time	Almost always
1.1 Self-confidence.					
Copes with difficulties in managing anger.					
Appears worried about being able to manage anger.					
Overreacts when asked to manage his anger.					
Recognises own success at managing anger.					
Can be given responsibility for managing own anger.					
1.2 Self-awareness.					
Can discuss difficulties in managing own anger.					
Can express feelings about own anger management appropriately.					
Denies having difficulties about need for own anger management.					
1.3 Friendships.					
Has difficulties making friends.					
Has difficulties maintaining friendships.					
Tends to follow other pupils.					
Tends to dominate other pupils.					
1.4 Managing disagreements with peers.					
Gets into lots of disagreements.					
Disagreements often end in a fight.					
1.5 Awareness of others' needs.					
Seems only concerned about self.					
Can listen to others.					
Helpful to staff.					
Helpful to peers.					
Shows insight into others' situations.					
1.6 Responding to correction.					
Overreacts.					
Responds well and changes behaviour.					
Accepts correction with difficulty.					

An Anger Management Checklist for Staff (Cont)

2. Behaviour	1	2	3	4	5
	Hardly ever	Sometimes	About half the time	Much of the time	Almost always
2.1 Interactions with peers.					
Physically aggressive.					
Finds it difficult to join in.					
Gets picked on.					
Teased.					
2.2 Interactions with adults.					
Physically aggressive.					
Verbally aggressive.					
Withdrawn.					
Attention-demanding.					
Provocative.					
2.3 Movement about the class.					
Wanders about the class when angry.					
Interferes with others when angry.					
Leaves the room when angry.					
2.4 Pupil noise when angry.					
Constantly talks to peers.					
Shouts out.					
Interrupts teacher.					
Makes non-verbal noises (for example, tapping pencil).					
2.5 Behaviour in other areas of school (for example, corridors, playground, main office) when angry.					
Physically aggressive to staff.					
Physically aggressive to pupils.					
Verbally aggressive to staff.					
Verbally aggressive to pupils.					
Unintentionally interferes with others.					
Intentionally interferes with others.					
Misuses and/or vandalises equipment.					
Engages in graffiti.					

	1 Much worse	2 Worse	3 Average	4 Better	5 Much better
3. How does the pupil's ability to manage their anger compare with others in the class/year group?					

Chapter 3: Teacher Skills Necessary to Implement a Whole-School Approach to Anger Management

The essential elements of good teacher planning are to be on time, well prepared, able to provide an appropriately differentiated curriculum to meet all pupil needs and the ability to treat pupils with respect. For effective learning to take place pupils must be on time, bring the required equipment, follow instructions, co-operate with staff and peers and work to achieve their full potential. These elements and requirements form the basis of teacher and pupil responsibilities respectively.

Rules and Routines

Rules are the mechanism by which rights and responsibilities are translated into adult and pupil behaviours. Rules give formal protection to rights and responsibilities. The general purpose of a rule is to make life easier and better for the majority of the school community.

Guidance for the formation of rules:

- Have a maximum of five, phrased briefly, succinctly and positively, stating what you need pupils to be doing (that is to learn) and not what you want them to stop doing (that is to unlearn).

- Discuss and possibly negotiate the rules with the pupils, although the classroom is not a democracy and you may end up manipulating suggestions made by the class.

- Keep the rules alive through frequent reference and bold display.

- Discuss rules within the department and/or year group and come to some agreement as this helps create a consistent approach.

- Rules like 'show respect' are too abstract. Ask yourself the question: what would I see pupils doing or hear them saying if they were 'showing respect'? This helps to form rules that are easy to understand, to keep, where pupils demonstrate positive behaviour and the teacher teaches it.

- Use inclusive language such as 'we will…'

- Never use 'always' or 'never' as nobody is perfect, we do our best.

Another way of formulating rules is to use the table below where an example is provided:

Rule	Reason for the rule	What will you see the pupil doing?
1. Follow teachers instructions at first time of asking.	Avoids confusion; prevents arguments or disagreements; ensures pupils are safe.	Stopping what they are doing when the teacher asks them to listen to what he has to say. Looking at the teacher when he is speaking.
2.		

Routines provide a structure to support teaching and learning and effective routines are clear and explicit, simple to follow and possible to teach. Clear routines that are well taught will help pupils to avoid losing their temper and free the teacher to teach. So, for example, a routine for late arrival to class will teach pupils the behaviour required when entering the classroom. This will enable the teacher to continue teaching whilst dealing with the late arrival with the minimum disruption. If the pupil is prone to becoming agitated and losing his temper if he is not noticed when he arrives, the teacher needs to do the following:

- Identify a spare desk in a convenient space in the classroom.

- Provide a pen and paper on the desk.

- Attend to the late arriving pupil at the earliest opportunity to avoid a possible temper tantrum and ensure involvement in the lesson.

- Teach and provide opportunities for pupils to practice the routine.

The pupil needs to do the following:

- Go straight to the 'late desk' on entering the classroom during a lesson.

- Write an explanation for the lateness on the paper provided.

- Attend to the lesson and wait for the teacher.

Why are Rules and Routines Important?

Routines underpin rules and reinforce classroom order and they may vary between teachers, subject areas and key stages of the national curriculum. Routines guide pupil behaviour within the classroom and are a way of providing certainty within busy classrooms with increased structure and opportunities for success for both staff and pupils. They are especially relevant where more than one adult is in a classroom and where pupils experience difficulties with communication and controlling their anger. However, it is important that routines are regularly reviewed and evaluated for their effectiveness.

Clear rules and routines enable pupils to carry out their responsibilities and enjoy their rights. Pupils will make choices about their responsibilities such that resulting consequences will be either positive or negative. Positive consequences such as rewards should be the result of pupils making responsible choices. Rewards acknowledge when pupils make good choices about their behaviour and help build self-esteem and positive relationships: they should be specific, appropriate, measured and genuine, and should motivate pupils to continue to choose appropriate behaviour. This is because pupils learn how to manage their anger best when they experience positive recognition and positive recognition is the key to changing behaviour because social approval encourages pupils to repeat the appropriate behaviours that are being taught.

However, should pupils choose to behave inappropriately, such as having a temper tantrum or outburst of anger, they will view a negative response as unfair and this is the inevitability of a negative consequence or sanction. Sanctions should be the stated or negotiated outcomes related to an inappropriate behaviour. They should be certain, inevitable, fair and appropriate, and not humiliate. They should occur when a pupil makes inappropriate behaviour choices and there should be links to more specific pupil support which can assist pupils further (for example, an individual behaviour plan that might include a behaviour contract say for anger management). Remember that staff disapproval is usually a powerful negative consequence say when a pupil's behaviour is becoming aggressive. Staff can invite pupils to think of ways of 'putting things right' instead of getting angry. The more sparingly consequences are used the more effective they are.

Key points in managing a crisis such as physical displays of anger:

- Ensure that the most severe consequences are used for the most severe displays of anger.

- Crisis plans need to be agreed, communicated and made explicit for the whole staff.

- Colleague back-up must not be seen as a sign of individual staff weakness but as part of a collegial support framework.

- Recording of serious incidents of physical or verbal aggression enables schools to inform parents and staff and review behaviour policy.

- Staff involved in an initial incident must also be involved in follow-up action.

Discussing Inappropriate (Angry) Behaviour with Pupils.

A facilitator might ask a whole-staff training group to provide him with answers to the question: what style of conversation usually takes place when a member of staff discusses a pupil's inappropriate loss of temper? The following points should be elicited during the discussion:

- Usually the member of staff does most of the talking.

- The pupil is told what they are doing wrong.

- If the pupil is complacent the member of staff can move off the point and drag up previous temper tantrums often from months before and thus becomes more and more angry himself by saying, 'And another thing...'

- It can become personal. 'You're just like your brother, he was a nuisance too.'

- The conversation often ends with the member of staff setting the targets, 'Right Harti, this is what you need to do,' followed by a list of behaviours. The pupil may agree to the targets just to end the conversation.

- The staff member asks the pupil why they did something.

- The member of staff uses 'you' messages, 'You are a nuisance.'

- The member of staff may not model appropriate behaviour.

- The pupil is not involved in setting targets to help put things right.

- The staff member may not offer the pupil suggestions for changing their behaviour.

- The staff member may not leave a 'way out' for the pupil to save face.

- The conversation may take place in public.

The facilitator may then want to obtain and record alternatives to the above list using the title: Staff Communication Skills – Strategies for avoiding and defusing confrontation. The list might include:

- Reference the Classroom Behaviour Plan regularly as this depersonalises issues and reminds pupils that they are responsible for their own behaviour choices.

- Provide reminders of rules and routines in a neutral tone.

- Acknowledge positive behaviour.

- Use inclusive language such as, 'In our school we…' as this encourages a sense of belonging.

- Allow pupils time to reflect on what you are asking or saying.

- Focus on pupils making choices as this reminds them that they are responsible for their own behaviour.

- Controll your own feelings by remaining calm.

- Remember that there are no guarantees that strategies will work and so if things do not change then try something else.

- Use humour based on positive relationships, not sarcasm.

Staff also need to ensure that a calm atmosphere is maintained in order to help sustain positive relationships. Problems may occur for individual staff however if whole-school systems are not in place to support staff when 'angry' pupils have been removed from the classroom.

For whole-staff training the facilitator might want to invite a staff group to discuss in groups of six to eight which aspects of the 4Rs Framework are already in place in their own classrooms. The small groups can record their comments on flipchart paper for display so that all participants of the training session have an opportunity to read others' ideas.

Examples of good practice of the 4Rs framework would include:

- Positively phrased rules.

- Including pupils in rule making.

- Routines that promote an orderly atmosphere.

- Logical and inevitable consequences for behaviour.

The facilitator should explain to training participants that behaviour planning in the classroom should be designed to support the development of the necessary positive behaviour skills required of pupils within the 4Rs framework. And that in any class there will be pupils who will respond to the social environment and engage with teacher encouragement for them to learn in a number of different ways. For example, pupils may be intrinsically engaged and motivated to learn to express and manage their feelings, even so they will still need some positive encouragement in each lesson. It is possible to give these pupils less attention and they may not cause any problems for the teacher.

Such pupils are likely to be academically successful and popular with their peers and they can be described as keen learners. Positive feedback will encourage them to continue working, behaving well and will motivate other pupils to have high expectations for themselves. As teachers, we need to keep these pupils on our side. Whereas receptive learners (the majority of the class group), will be influenced by both peers and teacher behaviour. Teachers need to provide receptive learners with interesting, challenging and stimulating lessons together with positive recognition of their achievements in controlling their anger. Teachers need to ensure that receptive learners are kept feeling positive, motivated and fully involved as members of the class.

In contrast, there will be a group of passive learners who may be disaffected, gifted or talented, irregular attendees or bored and who may have experienced some learning difficulties, such that school is not easy for them. Passive learners have the potential to be positive and to become receptive or even keen learners or to become disruptive, say through angry outbursts, and see themselves as completely outside the class group, joining the at risk pupils.

Passive learners can be easily influenced by the 'at risk' pupils and it is essential to explore what motivates them to respond positively to teaching and to consider how to listen to them and build positive relationships. This is because pupils who feel they do not belong to the class or the school are likely to require additional support. These 'at risk' or disengaged learners are more of a classroom management problem in that they require a whole-school approach.

The facilitator would then ask the same small staff groups to think about a class they currently teach or support and how many pupils they would allocate to each of the four categories described (that is, keen learners, receptive learners, passive learners and disengaged learners) and to consider what components within the classroom ethos might be influential in pupils belonging to each group. The activity page 'Categories of Learners' (page 54) could be used for this task.

The same small groups would then be asked to generate a list on a flipchart of specific examples that they consider are a positive influence in their classrooms to be shared amongst the whole group. The facilitator could compare the generated lists with the information below. Pupils learn how to control their anger best when:

- they are secure, happy, welcomed and simulated within the classroom environment

- they are seen to be valued

- they are feeling confident

- they are familiar with classroom rules and routines

- there are clear expectations and explanations

- there are purposeful, challenging and motivating activities and tasks

- a positive approach is used and fun is promoted

- they feel they are improving their skills

- the teacher is supportive and provides guidance.

The facilitator would explain to participants that building on the 4Rs framework and classroom dynamics of 'learner-types' descriptions and interactions is essential in order to teach pupils how to meet our expectations of behaviour in the classroom. An effective classroom behaviour plan should outline the clarity, structure, encouragement and motivation required to meet our expectations of pupil behaviour. Within such a classroom ethos pupils are more likely to be attracted to teacher encouragement for learning to manage their anger.

The facilitator would then invite the small groups to discuss briefly their own plan for managing classroom behaviour and how it is structured, then collect and record a sample of ideas from the groups on a flipchart.

Some possible responses to this activity might include the following statements:

- I have no classroom behaviour plan.

- I know how I want the pupils to behave but do not plan this.

- This is part of the pastoral, departmental or key stage planning process.

- We already have a whole-school approach to behaviour plans.

- All NQTs receive induction in classroom behaviour planning.

To which the facilitator might remind participants that:

- It is important to be consistent in the principles of a positive behaviour management approach as teachers are not clones or robots and have different ways of doing things.

- There will be some differentiation within routines and in positive feedback approaches.

- Good rules will be generally consistent across departments and year groups.

- Collegial support enables the most effective delivery of whole-school behaviour management approaches.

A classroom behaviour plan should incorporate the rules, routines and consequences, both positive and negative, for pupil behaviour. So, for example, the plan may include the following:

Rules (expectations)	Incentives (positive recognition of appropriate behaviour choices)	Consequences (negative outcome for poor behaviour choices)
<ul><li>Maximum of five.</li><li>Positively phrased (that is, what do we want pupils to do?).</li><li>Succinct and clear.</li><li>Based on observable, teachable behaviours.</li></ul>For example:<ul><li>Follow instructions.</li><li>Speak politely to others.</li><li>Take care of our classroom and each other.</li><li>Work quietly and do your best.</li><li>Raise hands and wait to speak.</li></ul>	<ul><li>Acknowledge when pupils make good choices about their behaviour.</li><li>Build self-esteem and positive relationships.</li><li>Motivate pupils to choose appropriate behaviour.</li><li>Range through non-verbal, social, tangible, individual, class-wide and school-wide.</li></ul>For example:<ul><li>Praise (both verbal and non-verbal).</li><li>Positive notes and comments.</li><li>Certificates.</li><li>Privileges, such as choice of activity, special responsibilities.</li></ul>	<ul><li>Occur when pupils make inappropriate behaviour choices.</li><li>Are certain, inevitable, fair, appropriate, will not humiliate and do not need to be severe.</li><li>Enable positive relationships to be maintained.</li><li>Involve collegial support.</li></ul>For example:<ul><li>Disapproval, redirection to task, rule reminder.</li><li>Warning.</li><li>Internal relocation.</li><li>Detention at the end of the lesson.</li><li>Working in another class.</li><li>Parental contact.</li><li>Senior management contact.</li></ul>

So a classroom behaviour plan is the process through which a teacher teaches the 4Rs framework. All teachers should know how they would like pupils to behave in their classrooms and will already have strategies for dealing with appropriate and inappropriate behaviour such as temper tantrums. However, not all teachers will have clear, well thought out structures for their behaviour management approaches. And many teachers will not have considered how to teach appropriate behaviour to their pupils. We must make the assumption that pupils do not know how to behave well because no-one has taught them yet. Positive behaviours need to be both directly taught and opportunities provided for them need to be rehearsed regularly. Such logic is used for all other curriculum areas and we have much to gain from applying such approaches to teaching behaviour.

The Impact of Classroom Dynamics

The interactions and relationships between pupils and staff, pupils and their peers, and staff with each other all impact on teaching and learning in the classroom. These relationships will also be changing throughout the day as additional influences come into play, for example, in curriculum subject areas, teaching approaches and styles and the composition of different class groups as well as classroom layout. The way in which people relate to each other and to the learning environment can be called the classroom dynamic and many variables contribute to the dynamics of the classroom, including:

- the time of day
- the nature of the previous lesson or break/lunchtime
- the weather
- the time within the school term or year
- a news event
- how people are feeling
- the relationships between people.

The characteristics of these positive relationships will include genuine interest, trust, active listening, respect, open dialogue, understanding and empathy.

A facilitator would ask the staff group to work in pairs using the activity page, 'How are the Positive Relationships Characterised within the Class' (page 55), to consider a class currently taught or supported where they feel the dynamic has a positive influence on learning and anger management. Specific examples of how the characteristics of positive relationships are in evidence should be recorded

The activity page, 'Factors that Effect Classroom Dynamics for Managing Behaviour' (page 56) could be used as a supplementary activity.

By tracking a group of pupils across a school day it is possible to see how the dynamic changes depending on the following factors:

1. The people in the group and their roles and responsibilities:

- Staff-pupil relationships are enhanced when, for example, pupils are secure, happy, welcomed and stimulated within the classroom and school environment. Pupils need to feel that they are valued and they need to feel confident about themselves and their learning. Teaching needs to be purposeful and challenging and should be accompanied by activities and tasks that are motivating for pupils. Relationships are helped by familiar classroom rules and routines and where clear expectations and explanations are given, where teachers are supportive and provide guidance such that pupils feel that they are improving.

- The degree to which rules and routines have been established.

Rules and routines guide pupil behaviour within the classroom environment (for example, for entry into the classroom) and are a way of providing certainty through increased structure and opportunities for success for both pupils and teachers. Rules and routines are especially relevant where more than one adult works in the classroom and where pupils experience difficulties with communication.

2. The lesson:

- Does the teacher accommodates a range of behaviours?

This will be in the context of planned consequences for appropriate behaviour (that is, incentives and rewards) as well as for inappropriate behaviour such as loss of temper. Planning the consequences that pupils will receive as a result of appropriate or inappropriate choices and making these explicit ensures that the teaching environment remains calm and orderly and that pupils are treated fairly. This means that the teacher differentiates when applying consequences to meet the needs of individual pupils and therefore pupils learn to take responsibility for their own behaviour and to make positive behaviour choices.

- Is the learning is appropriately paced and differentiated?

Learning rather like behaviour has to be differentiated to meet individual needs and this is the responsibility of the teacher in conjunction with other school staff with a view to helping pupils eventually become independent learners.

3. The classroom ethos:
- Are rights and responsibilities respected?
- Are contributions valued?
- Are pupils and staff listened to?

Working within the 4Rs framework enables pupils to explore the fairness of positive behaviour management. Establishing a classroom behaviour plan ensures that adults are clear about their expectations of pupil behaviour and are able to use a consistent approach such that the classroom environment is secure and positive, and pupils are supported in their efforts. However, it is important that pupils learn to take responsibility for their own behaviour and by using a language of choice we are encouraging them to understand that they are in control of themselves and they can change the way they behave (for example, managing their temper better).

Incentives and positive recognition are elements of a classroom behaviour plan that can help change behaviour. It is important that we plan incentives that motivate pupils to make good choices (for example, stop and think before hitting out). For poor behaviour choices (for example, throwing a temper tantrum for not getting their own way), negative consequences are inevitable and essential: they should be planned, fair and consistently applied. Support from senior school leaders for classroom and subject teachers is an important part of the process of staff being listened to. Using positive language in the classroom and amongst staff managing children's 'angry' behaviour, promotes an ethos in which pupils and staff feel valued and respected. Pupils will be more willing and able to comply with teacher requests and develop a feeling of belonging to the class group. Staff will be more willing to work with senior leader ideas and develop a feeling of belonging to the school.

If this was undertaken as a supplementary activity the facilitator could ask staff to work in pairs to consider a class or group they teach or support where any of the above issues have a positive or negative influence on the classroom dynamic in terms of preventing or successfully managing behaviour with particular reference to controlling anger.

Rather than take feedback from the staff pairs, the facilitator may want to ask staff to follow up this activity individually with a personal reflection on the relationships they have developed with the classes currently taught or supported and to follow-up this reflection with a colleague or mentor to identify good practice and build new approaches. The table below might act as a guide to personal reflection and for discussions with a colleague or mentor.

How Can Staff Support the Needs of Pupils in the Classroom?

Pupils need to	Teaching behaviour
• be working in a well-organised classroom	Make explicit expectations of behaviour for learning. Support all pupils in meeting expectations.
• feel they are responsible for managing their own behaviour	Negotiate rules and routines with pupils. Encourage responsibility through offering pupils choice.
• feel they are listened to and that their ideas are valued	Plan opportunities for pupils to discuss and share their ideas. Incorporate agreed pupil suggestions.
• feel successful and confident that they are making progress in controlling their anger	Praise pupils appropriately for their progress. Address pupils' approach to anger management. Involve pupils in self and peer monitoring of their behaviour.
• feel they belong to the class group	Treat all pupils with respect. Consistently apply the behaviour plan and/or policy.

Remember that anger is often at the root of dysfunctional behaviour in schools and so try to encourage and support staff in the following:

- Avoid greeting pupils' anger with your own because a pupil who is losing or has lost control needs a calm and rational approach from an adult.
- Avoid 'blowing hot and cold' in your response to pupil anger because pupils need to understand about your displeasure about their behaviour.
- Offer pupils the chance to talk about how they are feeling.
- Encourage pupils to recognise their own strengths.
- Use genuine and specific praise about pupils' positive behavioural choices.

In reflecting on your current whole-school systems for positive recognition you may want to consider the following questions:

- How effective are the incentives for individual pupils and whole classes?
- How accessible are they to all pupils?
- How are pupils involved in developing incentive programmes?
- How meaningful are they to all pupils?
- How are they differentiated by year groups or key stages?
- For which particular aspects of anger management are they awarded?

3

Summary

This chapter considers the necessary teacher skills for implementing the 4Rs framework together with an introduction to the classroom dynamics between the different types of learners and the factors that might affect the dynamics. Classroom behaviour plans and the development of positive classroom relationships are discussed.

Questions for You to Consider

- Are you happy with the way in which staff have formulated the classroom rules and routines? If not, how might you encourage staff to adopt more suitable ones to help better manage or prevent children from getting angry?
- In what ways could you use the 4Rs framework to help staff improve or further develop their classroom behaviour plans?
- How might you encourage staff to make use of the classroom dynamics to improve staff and pupil relationships?

Categories of Learners

Category	Number of pupils	Components within the classroom that might be influential within this category
Keen learners		
Receptive learners		
Passive learners		
Disengaged learners		

How are the Positive Relationships Characterised within the Class?

Characteristics of Positive relationships	Pupil-pupil	Pupil-staff	Staff-staff
Genuine interest			
Trust			
Active listening			
Respect			
Open dialogue			
Understanding			
Empathy			

Chapter 3

Factors that Effect Classroom Dynamics for Managing Behaviour (Particularly Controlling Anger)

Factors that affect the classroom dynamic	Does this factor have a positive or negative influence?	Note any actions that may positively influence the dynamic of the group
The People		
Staff roles and responsibilities		
Pupil-pupil relationships		
Pupil-staff relationships		
Staff-staff relationships		
Pupil self-confidence		
Pupil access to learning		

Factors that Effect Classroom Dynamics for Managing Behaviour (Particularly Controlling Anger) (cont)

Factors that affect the classroom dynamic	Does this factor have a positive or negative influence?	Note any actions that may positively influence the dynamic of the group
The Lesson		
Established routines		
Different learning styles		
Differentiated learning		
The Classroom Ethos		
Respect for rights and responsibilities		
Pupils and staff are listened to		
Contributions are valued		
Pupil response to teaching and management styles		

Chapter 4: The Cognitive Behavioural Approach: The Firework Model and the Storm Metaphor

It has been suggested that one of the most effective approaches to anger management is CBT. CBT has a good evidence base in terms of its effectiveness in reducing symptoms and preventing relapse (Spence at al. (2000), Clarke et al. (1999)). It has been recommended in the UK by the National Institute for Health and Clinical Excellence as a treatment of choice for a number of mental health difficulties, including post-traumatic stress disorder (PTSD), obsessive compulsive disorders (OCD), bulimia nervosa and clinical depression.

CBT most closely allies with the scientist-practitioner model of psychology, in which clinical practice and research is informed by a scientific perspective, clear operationalisation of the 'problem' or 'issue', an emphasis on measurement (and measurable changes in cognition and behaviour) and measurable goal-attainment.

The cognitive behaviour theorists believe that faulty thoughts and beliefs underlie anger problems. This is a two-pronged approach: firstly, decreasing the physiological arousal using relaxation procedure and secondly cognitive thought restructuring or simply changing how you think. Raymond Novaco (1975) developed a programme for helping adults to deal with anger and this has been modified for use with teenagers and children (Faupel et al., 1998).

The Firework Model

A firework has been used as a model to explain the way anger works (Faupel et al., 1998). This model has proven particularly accessible and memorable to children and young people during anger management groups. For example, grasping the idea of avoiding triggers such as people, situations, times or words, or else minimising or reducing their impact by being able to rethink or reframe their reaction to triggers by lengthening or extinguishing their fuses before an explosion.

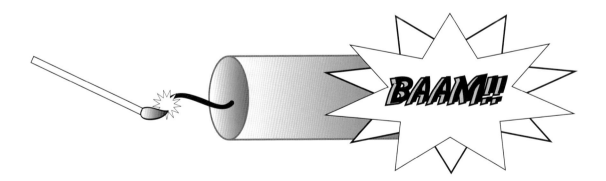

There are three components to the firework model:

1. Trigger.
2. Fuse.
3. Explosive firework.

The trigger is the match that lights the firework and sets off the anger response. The body of the firework is our reaction internally and externally to the event outside us, and the fuse is the mind or our thoughts about the event (Novaco, 1975). There are external factors and internal factors which contribute to the explosion. The external factors we may or may not have control over, for example, stress in the classroom – too hot, too many people, someone pushing into you. The internal factors we can control. These are our thoughts, which stem from a belief we hold. The other internal factor we can control is our physical reaction to a situation. How we interpret the event can make us angry or calm us down. Our internal response stems from our beliefs and expectations in certain situations, which triggers the internal dialogue we have in our own heads.

The trigger can be any of our five senses, person or situation specific and can be on any scale of severity. The fuse can be thoughts and feelings and these may or may not power up our anger. The fuse may be short or long and it can sometimes be cut or extinguished. The firework is the explosion which may be minor or devastating. Containment can reduce the impact on others and it is often advisable to remove other children if the explosion is too dangerous.

Fireworks and Storms

If the firework model is a schematic representation at the individual level, showing what happens when children get angry, then the metaphor of 'a storm' may help to describe anger in terms of the 'bigger picture' where environmental influences are as important as the reaction of the individual child.

The use of metaphor is a mental practice as old as philosophy and poetry. Sontag (1989) suggests that people cannot think without using metaphorical images. A metaphor is a figure of speech in which a word or a phrase that ordinarily designates one thing is used to designate another, thus creating an implicit comparison (Flexner, 1993). Metaphors use 'symbolic language' to 'uncover knowledge' that otherwise might be unrecognised. Metaphors, '…say a thing is or is like something it is not,' (Sontag, 1989). Metaphors intend to suggest, and reveal, certain images that enable us to see a likeness between initially different events and metaphors give us two ideas for one. Metaphors do not add facts to a description, rather they add depth of meaning to the nature of a phenomenon or experience. They provide a model of novel ways of looking at behaviour or thinking about a topic. They simplify events in the terms of a schema or concept that emphasises some properties more than others. They give communications an intimate or personal quality because of the concrete referents of metaphorical imagery (Lakoff & Johnson, 1980).

The storm metaphor is associated with Peter Sharp (2000) when he suggested that anger is like a storm: storms happen and they do not ask for permission. Sometimes you get a warning such as gathering clouds, changes in air pressure or wind direction, light fading or sudden darkness. And so it is with some angry outbursts or violent incidents. Avoidance strategies can help in trying to head off a storm or to go round it rather than through it. Some storms appear unannounced and both teachers and parents will sometime describe children's anger as appearing 'out of the blue'. And so there is a need to weather the storm, defuse the anger at the point of difficulty before the angry outburst becomes too dangerous. Storms are inevitable and so strategies for clearing up after the storm and learning from the experience as well as planning to reduce the likelihood of a similar storm are needed.

Weathering the Storm – the Assault Cycle

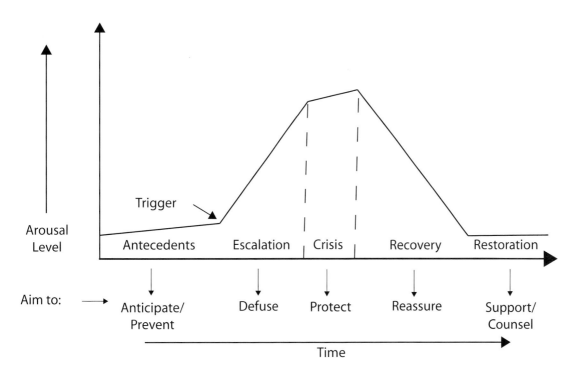

Adapted from A. Arnett 1987

There are five phases to the assault cycle:

1. The antecedents/trigger phase.

This is related to the firework model in which a child's fuse may be ignited, stimulating thoughts and feelings which can lead to displays of anger as a result of, for example, threats to self-esteem or self-image and threats to personal safety or property.

2. The escalation phase.

This is when the body is preparing 'physiologically' for a 'fight or flight' response: there is usually an adrenaline rush, muscles tense with rapid breathing and raised blood pressure. It equates with a shortening of the firework fuse.

3. The crisis phase.

This is where the child is unable to make rational judgements or is unable to demonstrate empathy with others. This is where the firework is exploding.

4. The plateau or recovery phase.

This is where the child's anger begins to subside. It usually takes time for the body to return to normal and it is easy for the anger to escalate again if there is an inappropriate adult intervention because the child's body is still partly prepared for action and the child is likely to be feeling particularly vulnerable and confused at this stage.

5. The restoration phase.

This is where the child's body needs to rest and recover from its high state of arousal. It is usually the stage at which the child is able to listen and think clearly. The child may then begin to feel guilty.

The early warning signs for the onset of the cycle can begin with physical agitation such as pacing up and down, fiddling with equipment and twitching legs. A change in facial expression, eye contact, body posture, tone of voice, position in the classroom accompanied by rapid mood swings is likely. There may be verbal challenges and over-sensitivity to suggestions or criticisms.

Unhelpful and devaluing comments, especially at the plateau or recovery stage include: 'Pull yourself together,' 'I thought you were more grown up than this,' 'Don't be silly!' 'Don't start that again!'

Children may go through this cycle in a matter of minutes, hours, days or weeks.

The key to intervention is teaching new skills, putting a strategy in place to deal with the behaviour as it occurs, not reinforcing the inappropriate or aggressive behaviour and reinforcing the student in using appropriate ways to communicate and get what they want. If a student has difficulty in a subject area we teach to it. In the same way if a student has a problem controlling his or her anger we should teach to this also. Therefore to intervene with a student who has difficulties with anger management we must first teach relaxation procedures. Next, we have to help the student to understand that there are external events that he may have no control over, but that he can control how he thinks about them or how he physically reacts to any given situation by explaining anger in terms of the fireworks analogy and being aware of the phases within the assault cycle. The next stage is to help students track their thoughts and anger, to become aware of triggers and signs. The interventions discussed thus far: problem-solving, conflict resolution and relaxation have wider applications. These are life skills which are relevant for all students and not just those with problems controlling anger. Finding the time to teach these skills can be a challenge but thirty minutes of prevention is better then two hours of fire fighting. A proactive approach is better then a reactive one.

Some Helpful Staff Behaviours for Managing Fireworks and Storms

1. The match – strategies to avoid the escalation stage:

   - Get in quick and be positive.

   - Divert the child onto something else.

   - Tell the child what you want them to do not what you don't want them to do.

   - Avoid 'trigger situations'.

   - Give time for the child to comply.

2. The fuse is lit – strategies to avoid the crisis stage:

   - Help the child to make a good choice about 'fight or flight'.

   - Watch for signs (tenseness, breathing, facial expressions) and remove the child or others from the situation.

   - Stay calm and do not provoke the child.

3. Strategies for dealing with the explosion:

   - Make things safe – remove dangerous objects and get others to leave.

   - Use physical restraint only if the child is a danger to themselves or others – check local authority policy and procedures around restraint guidelines.

- Stay in control and do not make matters worse by using imitation or ridicule, for example.
- Get help. Do not be proud, be smart.

4. Strategies for working through the recovery phase:
- Do not ask provocative questions.
- Allow time for recovery – the child and you.
- Guide the child towards something you would like them to do.
- Consider the use of a 'time out' tactic – exit cards for example.

5. Getting beyond the restoration stage:
- Do not try to load the child with more guilt.
- If there was anything positive to praise then go for it! (For example, say well done for avoiding hitting.)
- Discuss how to change the behaviour in the future in a positive and caring way. (For example, 'If you feel that angry again, use your exit card.')

Planning to Avoid Storms at School

This requires strong leadership in identifying anger management as a priority component of a school's behaviour policy. Within the behaviour policy there will need to be senior leadership team support to ensure consistency of practice between and amongst staff. An attractive school environment within an atmosphere that encourages shared values and staff cohesiveness are essential ingredients. Staff must set high expectations for behaviour and achievement for all pupils irrespective of their learning and behaviour needs. Classroom environments need to be relatively predictable with gradual or evolutionary change to support consistency of practice between and amongst staff. There must be a clear focus on teaching and learning of anger management strategies with a concomitant reduction in inappropriate competition and confrontation.

Pupils need extrinsic (that is tangible) and intrinsic (that is social praise) incentives to succeed and to share responsibility for learning and participation in the life of the school. Parental involvement and extra-curricular activities are also essential building blocks for success.

In considering some approaches for developing whole-school policies, consistent teacher behaviour and creating a positive temperament amongst staff to generate an appropriate school ethos we can draw on some ideas from 'solution focused or orientated approaches'.

The ten principles of solution focused or orientated approaches are:

1. If it works, do more of it; If it doesn't work, then do something different.
2. A small change in any aspect of a problem or failed solution can initiate a new solution.
3. People have the necessary resources to make changes.
4. A focus on future possibilities and solutions enhances change.
5. No sign up – no change.

6. Co-operation enhances change.

7. The problem is the problem, not the person.

8. Possibilities are infinite.

9. People have unique ways of solving their problems.

10. Keep one foot in pain and one in possibility (that is, be aware of problems as well as their possible solutions).

With solution orientated approaches you can:

- identify strengths, competencies and exceptions
- share information and learn from colleagues in an interactive setting
- ask and answer questions
- discuss important issues and reach decisions as a group
- coordinate the joint efforts of individuals within a team
- encourage and support reflective thinking
- tap into individual and team resources and experiences
- gain perspective on an issue
- encourage team building

The main techniques used with such approaches include: focusing on strengths, scaling, exceptions, preferred futures, action planning and goal setting.

Focusing on Strengths

Making use of strengths suggests that 'problem owners' have the necessary resources to change school problems and that a positive change may be made by utilising these strengths, skills and resources. It encourages a view of the problem as 'stuckness' rather than 'sickness' and seeks to use competencies to overcome problems.

At the end of the chapter there is an opportunity for staff to think and talk about their 'strengths'. The facilitator would ask pairs of staff to use the activity page 'Focusing on Strengths' (page 71) to think of a recent achievement that they are prepared to talk to each other about. The person in the pair listening to the description of that achievement would then ask a series of questions which could be recorded on the activity page and feed back to the larger staff group. The facilitator could then ask the whole staff group for any patterns or themes emerging from the small group feedback.

The purpose of carrying out this activity is that drawing on strengths, rather than focusing on problems or what is going wrong, is one of the first and basic tenets of solution orientated approaches. It enables the problem owner to realise that he has the skills to solve the problem based on previous successful experiences.

Eliciting competencies, strengths and successes provides opportunities for hearing about what:

- is going OK in relation to particular issues
- does not need changing
- can be kept
- can be expanded upon
- can be developed
- strengths and resources are present.

Scaling

Scales are a key tool in measuring change, charting the next small step, helping to evaluate and maintain progress, and encompassing every aspect of the solution-orientated approach. Scaling can also be used as a structured interview with individual pupils to negotiate staged or scaled interventions as described below.

Using 'Scaling Techniques' to Identify the Current and Possible Future Directions for Managing Angry Children

The following questions are asked of a child who has problems managing their anger.

- On a scale of 0-10 how do you rate any concerns that you have at school at the moment?
- Where would you put yourself at your worst point?
- How did you get from your worst point to the point you're at today?
- In your journey from your worst point to where you are today, what have you noticed about yourself?
- Who around you knew you'd get by?
- What did they see in you that reassured them that you would be OK?
- If you have not moved from your lowest point, how are you coping with the concern you have?
- What are you doing to keep yourself going?
- How will you know when you have moved one point along?

The scaling activity, 'Scaling: the Efficacy of Whole-School Approaches to Managing Angry Children' (page 72) can be used to consider where the school is at present and how things would look if approaches were improved.

Using the guide sheet, 'A 'Staged' Approach to Managing Difficult Behaviour' (page 73), pairs of staff should match low levels of behaviour (level 1) with the specific behaviours moving through the levels to level 5. Once completed, the pairs would consider the possible interventions required to address the difficult behaviour at each level. The facilitator could use the information from the sheets for a general whole-staff group discussion to formulate ideas for change.

Scaling can be put in the context of a possible 'behavioural continuum' in the 'staged approach to managing difficult behaviour' by obtaining similarities and differences amongst staff as to what constitutes difficult to manage behaviour and what might be the possible interventions. A behaviour continuum may look something like this:

Level	Some examples of 'difficult' behaviour
1	Shouting out answers in class. Calling out to other pupils across the classroom during work activities.
2	Shouting out answers in class – despite reminders to raise hand and wait to be asked. Calling out to other pupils across the classroom during work activities – despite verbal reminders/reprimands.
3	Continued shouting out of answers in class – despite frequent verbal and visual reminders to raise hand and wait to be asked (that is, part of classroom rules pinned up on wall). Continued calling out to other pupils across the classroom during work activities – despite having to complete work at break and lunchtimes.
4	Persistent shouting out of answers in class – despite frequent verbal and visual reminders to raise hand and wait to be asked (that is, classroom rules pinned up on wall). Persistent calling out to other pupils across the classroom during work activities – despite having to complete work at break and lunchtimes.
5	Persistent shouting and calling out and a serious physical attack on another pupil at lunchtime.

Level	Some examples of 'difficult' behaviour	Possible interventions
1	Shouting out answers in class. Calling out to other pupils across the classroom during work activities.	Verbal reminders to raise hand and wait to be asked. Verbal reminders/reprimands.

The small groups can then share their grids as a whole group and the facilitator then works with the whole staff group to arrive at consensus for both the graduated levels of difficult behaviour and the appropriate interventions for each level.

The purpose of this activity is to obtain staff opinions on the levels they would associate with particular behaviours and, when the small groups feed back to the whole staff group, to obtain consensus about what behaviours can be associated with particular levels and what would constitute an appropriate intervention for each level.

Level one would be considered low and level five as high with the idea that interventions should be similarly graduated to match the level of behaviour in that, for example, you would not necessarily take a hammer to crack a walnut. The table produced in the activity should be copied onto flipchart paper for recording and feedback purposes.

Exceptions

Proponents of solution-orientated approaches insist that there are always times when the problem is less severe or absent. It is therefore helpful to encourage the problem owner to describe what different circumstances exist in that case, or what the problem owner did differently. The goal is to repeat what has worked in the past and to help the problem owner gain confidence in making improvements for the future. The questions used are described as 'exception-seeking'. So seeking exceptions are a means of looking at what happens differently when the problem (for example, child becoming angry) does not occur.

In parallel with exception questions are coping questions. Coping questions are designed to elicit information about the problem owner's resources that will have gone unnoticed by them. Even the most hopeless story has within it examples of coping that can be drawn out and a training group facilitator could adopt the following script with a member of staff who he knows has been having problems managing angry children:

'I can see that things have been really difficult for you yet I am struck by the fact that, even so, you manage to get up each morning and do everything necessary to get the kids off to school. How do you do that?'

Genuine curiosity and admiration can help to highlight strengths without appearing to contradict the problem owner's view of reality. The initial summary, 'I can see that things have been really difficult for you,' is for them true and validates their story.

The second part, 'You manage to get up each morning,' is also a truism but one that counters the problem-focused narrative. Undeniably, they cope and coping questions start to gently and supportively challenge the problem-focused narrative. The same script can be applied to staff working with individual or groups of children who have problems managing their anger and yet still come to school every day!

Preferred Futures

In contrast, the miracle question is a method of questioning that can be used to envision how the future will be different when the problem is no longer present. Also, this may help to establish goals. A traditional version of the miracle question would go like this:

'Suppose our meeting is over, you go home, do whatever you planned to do for the rest of the day. And then, sometime in the evening you get tired and go to sleep. In the middle of the night, when you are fast asleep, a miracle happens and all the problems that brought you here today are solved just like that. Because the miracle happened overnight you don't realise that a miracle has happened. When you wake up the next morning, what will have changed to make you realise that a miracle has happened? What else are you going to notice? What else?'

There are many different versions of the miracle question depending on the context and the problem. In a specific situation, you could ask, 'If you woke up tomorrow and a miracle had happened so that you no longer easily lost your temper, what would you see differently?' What would the first signs be that the miracle had occurred?'

The pupil may respond by saying, 'I would not get upset when somebody calls me names.'

You would want the pupil to develop positive goals, in terms of what they will do, rather than what they will not do in order to ensure success. So, you would ask the pupil, 'What will you be doing instead when someone calls you names?'

It is suggested that the miracle question is used with staff working in groups or it can be used by senior teachers mentoring staff one-to-one. It can also be used by staff with individual children who are having problems managing their anger.

The facilitator would ask staff to work in pairs. Both members of the pair should have a go at asking and answering questions from 'The Miracle Question' activity (page 74) based on the following script:

'Just imagine for a moment that you wake up tomorrow morning and a miracle has occurred while you were asleep and any concerns you had about school have disappeared.'

The facilitator would then ask both members of the same pairs to have a go at asking and answering the follow-up questions in the second part of this activity based on the following: 'If you were to pretend that the miracle had happened...'

Action Planning and Goal Setting

'Action planning' and 'goal setting' lay emphasis on the goals in the plan being do-able and being desirable, using the language of possibility and embodying confidence and a belief that you can make changes. There are two simple ways to arrive at goals:

1. Directly from the extension, development, evolution, mobilisation or utilisation of any strength or competency already noted.

2. By asking what is happening differently when the pupil is not angry.

Action planning and goal setting can be used by senior staff working with individual colleagues to help them in their approach to managing angry children.

The facilitator would ask the same pairs of staff to complete the 'Action Planning Grid Activity' (page 75) which provides a script for this together with a blank proforma.

'Consider any one or more of the things you noticed in answering the miracle question (for example, what would be the first thing you would do? What would it take to pretend that this miracle had happened?) and draw up a proposed action plan along the lines of:

- Who?

- Might do what?

- With what degree/type of support?

- By when?'

This activity is drawn from responses to the second part of the 'miracle question' activity, that is, where respondents say what would be the first thing they would do if the miracle had happened. So, for example, if the class came into the room at the start of each day, chose a reading book and sat down quietly to wait for the teacher to call the register, the first thing the teacher might do would be to incorporate this into a class behaviour and consequences chart. This might mean that for every set of desirable expected behaviours there was a positive consequence. In this example the consequence could be to finish the lesson early and play a class game before play. This is illustrated in the table below to assist staff in using the action-planning grid.

Who?	What actions?	What support?	By when?
Class teacher.	Draw up a class behaviour and consequences chart in conjunction with the class.	Year group leader to encourage all class teachers in the year group to draw up similar charts for their classes.	The end of the first half-term.

A planning chart such as the above can be applied to both primary and secondary staff: in a secondary school 'subject teacher' would replace class teacher if the plan was used in departments or a similar plan could be applied to form tutors in different year groups.

Summary

The most effective approach to anger management is a cognitive behavioural approach. A firework model has proven particularly useful when working with children and young people. The storm metaphor helps to explain why environmental influences are as important as the reaction of the individual. The assault cycle illustrates the phases involved in aggressive behaviour from the trigger phase (similar to the firework model) to the recovery or post-crisis depression phase.

Questions for You to Consider

- How can the three components of the firework model help staff have a better understanding of children's temper tantrums?

- What might you do to help staff develop the appropriate strategies for managing children's anger throughout the assault cycle phases?

- In what ways might your school adopt the principles of solution-orientated approaches?

You may also want to think about further training in solution-orientated approaches for your staff. You may want to ask staff who have attended any such courses to cascade their knowledge and skills gained from courses.

Focusing on Strengths

In pairs think of a recent achievement you would want to talk about to your partner.

- What strengths, skills and resources did you draw on?

- When did you notice that you had these skills, strengths and resources in the past?

- What tells you that you've always had the capacity to do this?

- Of all the people you know well, who would be the least surprised?

- What is it that they knew about you that others did not see?

Scaling: the Efficacy of Whole-School Approaches to Managing Angry Children

Use the rating scale of 0-10 (where '0' is extremely ineffective and '10' is highly effective at managing angry children as a whole school) to answer the following questions:

- Where would you put the school now?

- What makes you say (whatever the rating was) rather than a '0'?

- If a rating of '1' was given, what is preventing it from getting any worse?

- Where would you like the school to be?

- Where do you think the school should be?

- What would it take to move the school up one point?

- What would be the first thing you would notice if the school moved up a point?

- What would be the first thing the children would notice if the school moved up a point?

- What would be the first thing the parents/carers would notice if the school moved up a point?

A 'Staged' Approach to Managing Difficult Behaviour

Level	Difficult behaviour	Possible interventions
Low 1		
2		
3		
4		
High 5		

Miracle Question

Just imagine for a moment that you wake up tomorrow morning and a miracle has occurred while you were asleep and any concerns you had about school have disappeared.

- What will you notice that is different? About the school, about you, about those around you?
- Who would notice that the concerns have gone?
- What would they see you doing differently?
- What would you see them doing differently?
- What have you learned that might help you?
- Who around you knew you'd get by?
- What did they see in you that reassured them that you would be OK?

If you were to pretend that the miracle had happened:

- What would be the first thing you would do?
- What would it take to pretend that this miracle had happened?
- If you were to do that, what would be the first thing you would notice about yourself?
- Who would be the first person to notice the next day that something is different about you after the miracle?
- If you were to take these steps, what would you notice about your classroom that would be different?
- If you were to do something different what would be the first thing the children would notice?
- What would they do differently?
- What else would be different about your classroom?

Action Planning Grid Activity

Consider any one or more of the things you noticed in answering the miracle question. For example, What would be the first thing you would do? What would it take to pretend that this miracle had happened? Draw up a proposed action plan along the lines of:

- Who?
- Might do what?
- With what degree/type of support?
- By when?

Who?	What actions?	What support?	By when?

Chapter 5: Visual Imagery and Relaxation and the Use of Role-Play

Relaxation training is an essential part of an anger management programme. Anger is an emotional reaction to a set of circumstances or triggers. The trigger or stressful event is known as provocation. Anger can have positive functions or negative functions. Anger can be positive as it can make us become more assertive and stand up for ourselves, it can help us express tension and it can energise us and help us feel in control (Novaco, 1975). It has negative effects when it is used too frequently, when it leads to aggression, when it is too intense, when it disrupts relationships or when it dictates the way we feel all the time.

We need to keep in mind that the mismatch between a pupil's ability and the demands of the school situation can be stressful and may produce aggression and disruptive behaviour in some. Relaxation training can also be used as a de-escalating or prevention technique. It can be adopted as part of an anger management programme or a stress management or anxiety reduction programme with older pupils.

There are several main types of relaxation techniques, including:

Autogenic relaxation. Autogenic means something that comes from within you. In this technique, you use both visual imagery and body awareness to reduce stress. You repeat words or suggestions in your mind to help you relax and reduce muscle tension. You may imagine a peaceful place and then focus on controlled, relaxing breathing, slowing your heart rate or different physical sensations, such as relaxing each arm or leg one by one.

Progressive muscle relaxation. In this technique, you focus on slowly tensing and then relaxing each muscle group. This helps you focus on the difference between muscle tension and relaxation and you become more aware of physical sensations. You may choose to start by tensing and relaxing the muscles in your toes and progressively working your way up to your neck and head. Tense your muscles for at least five seconds and then relax for 30 seconds, and repeat.

Visualisation. In this technique, you form mental images to take a visual journey to a peaceful, calming place or situation. Try to use as many senses as you can, including smells, sights, sounds and textures. If you imagine relaxing at the ocean, for instance, think about the warmth of the sun, the sound of crashing waves, the feel of the grains of sand and the smell of salt water. You may want to close your eyes, sit in a quiet spot and loosen any tight clothing.

Other relaxation techniques include those you may be more familiar with, such as:

- Yoga.
- Tai chi.
- Music.
- Exercise.
- Meditation.
- Hypnosis.
- Massage.

5

Setting the Scene for Relaxation

Often teachers have postures they ask pupils to adopt as a way to calm things down. Asking the pupils to close their eyes and sit with their shoulders relaxed, their hands on the desk with palms facing upwards and their legs outstretched for a few minutes before beginning a lesson can relax the mood in the class.

Posture can be incorporated into drama as a key to teaching relaxation.

To model posture for a staff group the facilitator would begin by asking staff to notice their own hands and then with their neighbour discuss any details they have never noticed before. The facilitator should encourage staff to describe, compare and contrast their hands with each other. The facilitator can then ask for volunteers from the pairs to share some of their descriptions – these can be recorded on a flipchart.

The facilitator would then ask the staff to discuss in their pairs how they habitually sit, stand and walk. He should remind staff that if this activity is carried out with children, care should be taken to ensure that it is not done in any judgmental way. So staff would not say to a group of children, 'Do you notice that Dwayne is slouching?' Staff should be encouraged to describe the posture to children positively by drawing their attention to what they want and not what they don't want, for example, 'Do you notice that Lola has her head up and her shoulders back?'

When this activity is done with children they have the tendency to sit up straight as they recall past reprimands from parents and teachers. The facilitator would remind staff that the aim of this activity is not to force children to assume a posture that does not match how they are thinking or feeling but rather to help raise their awareness of how body posture and attitude are linked.

The facilitator would encourage staff (who can also encourage children) to notice their own postures, using a full length mirror and point out that mirrors can also be used to explore facial expressions.

As a development of this activity, the facilitator would ask for a volunteer to have a go at a role-play by being a student and then give the rest of the staff group a script which involves tension and anxiety, such as the following:

'This boy is about to get the results of his test but he does not think he did well. He is sitting in his seat waiting for the paper to come back from the teacher.'

The staff group have to tell the volunteer what posture to assume when he gets his results.

This is a great learning experience. It helps to develop awareness of body language and the relationship between our thoughts and feelings and how they can manifest physically in our bodies. Once again this is an activity that staff can use with their pupils.

Stress is part of life and having a healthy way to cope with stress is an important life skill. We all carry tension in our bodies. A certain amount of tension in our muscles helps us to function, walk, talk, eat and so on. When we are under pressure, we hold tension in certain areas of our bodies. Having the pupil identify where they hold tension in their body can clue them in to signs that they need to relax. With pre and early teens, use a drawing and have them mark the areas of the body where they experience stress with a pencil or marker.

An important component in creating highly challenging learning environments that are not stressful depends on how staff increase their control over their mental and physical states. This means accessing information using memory and imagination – Stephen Bowkett (1999) calls this 'systematic daydreaming'.

The facilitator would then check this out with a staff group, assuming that enough of them engage in daydreaming, by asking them to discuss in pairs the answers to the following questions:

- Do you like daydreaming?

- Why is that?

- What do you think children and young people think about daydreaming?

- What is the difference between daydreaming and thinking about your last holiday?

Staff can of course use this activity with children and young people and substitute the third and fourth questions above with the following questions:

- What do you think adults think about daydreaming?

- What is the difference between daydreaming and making up a story?

Music can be used as a tool to build a calm atmosphere or as background for a relaxation exercise. The facilitator may wish to play music prior to a staff training session. Two guided visualisation scripts are provided at the end of the chapter and these can be used as a relaxation technique with the whole group of young people. The facilitator should try these out with a staff group first as a basis for discussion about the merits of using guided visualisation in school.

The first activity later in the chapter provides an example of guided visualisation (the full version). It would be preferable for the facilitator to take staff through both the full and shortened versions of guided visualisation for comments on their preferences for use with children and young people. As an introduction to guided visualisation (both versions), staff and young people can be asked an open-ended general questions such as, 'What do you do to relax?' Children sometimes find the concept of relaxation quite difficult to comprehend and so other words associated with relax may have to be substituted. For example, words such as, 'feel good about yourself'. The responses to this introductory activity can be summarised and noted. And then the guided visualisation can be introduced.

The rationale for using relaxation techniques and guided visualisation is that the mind and body are interconnected. Changing how we think can change how we feel. Changing how we interpret events by re-scripting our internal dialogue is called cognitive or thought restructuring. In anger management training this means identifying 'hot thoughts' and replacing them with 'cool thoughts'. Hot thoughts make us more angry and cool thoughts are thoughts which calm us down.

Developing Activities to Help Children Relax

Faupel et al. (1998) have suggested the use of cue cards with a range of alternate behaviour or calming strategies including self-talk which involves the child recognising the early warning signs before anger develops and then using 'cool-it' thoughts, words and actions. This technique is likely to work best at the earliest stages of anger. And the combination of self-talk with controlled breathing (see introduction to the guided visualisation activities, page 84) is likely to be even more effective when coupled with statements such as, 'I can hack this.' Positive self-talk could include the following script for children and young people:

- 'I deserve to be liked by other kids.'
- 'I deserve to be liked by teachers.'
- 'I want to be liked by other kids.'
- 'I want to be liked by teachers.'
- 'I can be liked by other kids.'
- 'I can be liked by teachers.'

If children and young people want to change their lives they need to change how they think and change what they do. Self-help and personal change for children and young people starts with the realisation that the possibility of change is really in their own hands and the decision to do something about changing their lives rests with them. Young people's own self-belief is the key to successful life-change, achievement, contentment and happiness. Self-belief can develop in the mind with positive suggestions and visualisation about their futures which will, in turn, provide them with the determination to make successful changes to their lives.

Of course, just because we recognise that it is ultimately children and young people's responsibilities to change how they think and what they do, this does not mean that we as adults should relinquish our obligations for encouraging them to make such changes. As teachers we must remind young people of the importance and benefits of taking responsibility for their actions. We should try and find examples in our own lives or in the lives of the young people's peers, where taking responsibility for change has had positive outcomes and where not doing so has had negative consequences for them and may have had for others too.

Cool thoughts might include a script, when previous responses had been to get into a verbal argument or fight, along the lines of:

'It's not worth having an argument and I'm not gonna stay because I might end up in a fight and then get into trouble with my teachers and my mum so I'm gonna walk away.'

Another technique referred to by Faupel et al. (1998) is self-calming, which can be further enhanced by actions coupled with self-talk such as discrete finger counting using the thumb of right hand against the fingers and making a positive statement each time the thumb touches a finger of the left hand. You will note too that some self-calming statements are used in the next chapter for children and young people engaged in anger management groups.

A self-calming script for a pupil who is having problems with class work and who otherwise might have had a temper tantrum could go along the lines of:

'I feel frustrated and angry because I can't do it. It's so hard that if I'm not careful I will lose my temper and shout out, "I can't do this." I don't know whether to give it up or to give it another try. I could ask someone in my group if the teacher allows that. Or I could go and ask the teacher although I might need to put up my hand first though. I could also leave this question till later and go back to it. And if the teacher is gonna give unfinished work as homework then I could ask someone at home to help me.'

The suggestions above could be explored and extended in staff group training where the facilitator would ask staff to describe (in pairs) the kinds of 'cool thoughts' and self-calming techniques they use to diffuse their anger with pupils at school. These could be listed on a flipchart for use by staff and children and young people.

Role-Play as a Means of Illustrating how Conflict can Arise and What Alternatives are Possible for Diffusing and Resolving such Situations

Role-play offers the opportunity to explore, through spontaneous representation and carefully guided discussion, typical conflict situations. During the process, children and young people are helped to become sensitive to the feelings of the people involved, recognise the consequences of the choices they make, and explore the kinds of behaviours that are effective and socially acceptable. Perhaps the most important aspect of the role-playing process is the fact that children and young people, with the help of peers, gradually become conscious of the choices they typically make in conflict situations and begin to replace ineffective behaviours with effective ones.

5

The role-playing process and suggested scenarios can be incorporated with staff group training led by a facilitator who would divide the staff up according to the chosen scenarios. A whole-group discussion would follow to explore the merits of adopting role-play within the school and to agree on the use of such an approach with the pupils at school as described in the paragraphs that follow.

The role-playing process should follow a step-by-step process like this:

- A discussion topic is introduced by the teacher for the role-play. Palomares and Akin (1995) have used a range of themes along the lines of asking young people to describe a time, for example, when other people wouldn't listen to them, when the young person got blamed for something they didn't do, when other people were mad at the young person for something the young person had done and vice versa and when a young person took their anger with one person out on someone else. Any one or more of these themes could be used as a programme of role-plays around conflict resolution or one or two could be chosen to reflect the current situation or context.

The facilitator could then:

- Carry out a discussion on a chosen topic by asking for volunteers to share their experiences and feelings.

- Choose an incident to role-play that has a clear-cut moment of conflict, involves two or more people and is resolvable through the use of positive conflict resolution strategies (for example, using 'I' messages, no-blame approach, seeing problem from the other side). The volunteer story-teller(s) would be asked to repeat the incident.

- Ask the volunteers to role-play the incident to the point of conflict and use prompt when needed such as:

  - What expression would you have on your face?

  - What would you say and how would you say it?

  - How did the other person/people react to what you said or did?

  - How did you feel?

- Ask the staff group to suggest alternative responses to the conflict.

- Obtain consensus as to which alternative might work best.

- Ask the 'actors' to role-play the scenario from the beginning and to use the positive alternative chosen by the staff group.

- Evaluate the effectiveness of the response and the role-play process by asking the following questions:

  - What would children and young people learn from this process?

  - Which parts would children and young people find the most valuable?

  - How can practising alternative resolutions to real life conflict situations when they occur help children?

As a means of summarising all of the training within this chapter and providing links between anger and relaxation, the facilitator could ask staff to complete the activity page 'How the Firework Model Applies to Me When I Get Angry' (page 87) using the visual representation of the firework. He would ask staff to fill in the columns on the activity page. The columns are:

- Triggers.

- Thoughts and Feelings.

- Body Reactions.

The facilitator would then ask the staff group to work in twos or threes to write a role-play scenario based on the content of their firework model activity pages. One group of two or three would be invited to volunteer to act out their script and the facilitator would also ask staff observing the role-play what successful self-talk, cool thoughts, self-calming they use. There could be a final discussion about how the completion of the firework model activity and resulting role-play could be used with children and young people.

Summary

Relaxation training is an essential component of anger management interventions. The rationale for using relaxation techniques and guided visualisation is that the mind and body are interconnected – changing how we think can change how we feel about something. The key to anger management interventions is teaching new skills to children and young people and putting strategies in place to deal with behaviour as it occurs.

Questions for You to Consider

- What do you use to relax?

- How might you encourage staff to share any of their relaxation techniques with their pupils?

- How might you be able to link your suggested techniques to particular children or groups of children at potentially stressful times, such as preparing for examinations?

- How might you encourage staff to make good use of the role-play process, especially as a conflict resolution technique?

5

Guided Visualisation (Full Version)

Materials and Resources

Flipchart.
Paper.
Pens, pencils and markers.

As an introduction the group would be asked open-ended general questions such as, 'What do you do to relax?' The responses could be noted down on a flipchart to help with the visualisation.

The group should be asked to make themselves comfortable with their feet flat on the ground and about nine inches apart and then the following script can be used. The facilitator should read this slowly, leaving space between sentences for the participants to focus on their breathing, visualisation and relaxation.

'Close your eyes or lower your gaze. Breathe in slowly. Let your breath out slowly. Again: in... out... Again, even more slowly: in... out...

Try to imagine that your stresses, your anxieties, your deadlines, are rolling off your head, down your shoulders, down your arms, and falling away to the floor. Find a calm center inside yourself. Keep your eyes closed.
You are awakening from a deep, very restful sleep filled with delightful dreams. As you awaken, you see the sky, blue, sunny, white fluffy clouds above you in the distance. You are lying on your back in thick grass. Sitting up, you look around and notice you are sitting on a high hill. Around the top of the hill is a neatly trimmed hedge. You smell the grass, the flowers and the fresh breeze. You hear birds singing. Standing, you walk over to the hedge where you have noticed a white gate. Putting your hand on the latch, you lift it and pause – anything could be on the other side. You swing the gate open and begin walking down the path, each step taking you deeper into this new world.
You look down the hill and realise that everything you had wished for has happened: the best and highest hopes that you had for the future have all been realised.
As you sit on the top of the hill:

- What do you see?

- What do you hear?

- What do you smell?

You walk down the hill, further into this changed world:

- What do the people walking towards you look like?
- What are these people doing?
- How are children playing?
- Where are the older people?
- Where are people working?
- What else do you see?
- What do you hear? Voices? Animals? Running water? Engines? What else do you hear?
- Can you smell gardens? Cooking?
- What else can you smell?

As you wander through this place you look for something that is of interest; something that you particularly like, and find it. What do you do? How do you feel? Take ten minutes to fully explore what that something is.
When you are ready, open your eyes and draw a picture or a diagram, or verbally summarise this something that is of interest or something that you particularly like on the paper provided.'

Finally the group have to be brought back to the present and this can be done as follows:

'You are now walking back through the gate and back into the present time. When I count backwards from five you will awaken and be back in this room at this point in time.'

Guided Visualisation (Shortened Version)

As an introduction, the group would be asked open-ended general questions such as, 'What do you do to relax?' The responses could be noted down on a flipchart to help with the visualisation. The following script should be read slowly, with space left between sentences for the participants to focus on their breathing, visualisation and relaxation.

'Make sure you are sitting comfortably with your feet on the ground and your eyes shut (or gaze lowered).

Become aware of your breathing... Become aware of your chest rising and falling as you breathe in and breathe out. If you feel tension in any part of your body simply let it go as you breathe out. Concentrate on the word r-e-l-a-x.

We all have a special place where we like to go in order to r-e-l-a-x.

Imagine that you are in your special place.

Take some time to look around. Notice all the things that you can see. Notice what you can hear. You then reach out to touch things that are near you. You notice how relaxing it is to be in your special place and that this is making you feel happy and content. Your body is beginning to r-e-l-a-x. Spend a few minutes relaxing in your special place.

It is now time to leave your special place. Before you leave, turn round and take one last look before you go

When you are ready, open your eyes and come back into this room.'

How the Firework Model Applies to Me When I Get Angry

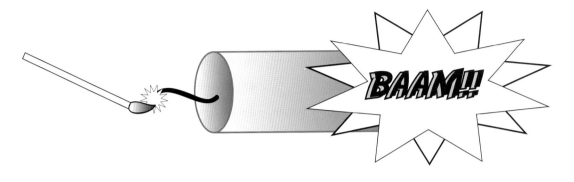

Triggers	Thoughts and Feelings	Body Reactions
....	....	....
....	....	....
....	....	....
....	....	....
....	....	....
....	....	....
....	....	....
....	....	....

Chapter 6: Preparing for an Anger Management Group Intervention Programme

Introduction

The theoretical basis for the group work detailed in this chapter is based on cognitive behavioural therapy (CBT) and builds on the application of CBT to the firework model described in Chapter 4. This approach enables us to talk about how we think of ourselves, the world and other people and how what we do affects our thoughts and feelings. It can help us to make sense of overwhelming problems by breaking them down into smaller parts. This makes it easier to see how they are connected and how they affect us. These smaller parts relate each difficult or problem situation to our thoughts, physical feelings, emotional feelings and actions. There are helpful and unhelpful ways of reacting to most situations, depending on how you think about them. Consider the following situation for example, 'You've had a bad day, feel fed up, and so you go out shopping. As you walk down the road, someone you know walks by and apparently he ignores you.'

An unhelpful thought about this situation would be that the person you know deliberately ignored you because he doesn't like you. Alternatively you could think that the person you know looked a bit wrapped up in himself and you might think that there is something wrong: this alternative thought is much more helpful than your first thought. This is because your first unhelpful thought is likely to make you feel low, sad and rejected. You might then experience stomach cramps and feel sick, and then go home as a means of avoiding the person you know. The second and more helpful thought is likely to make you feel concern for the person you know and you are unlikely to experience the same physical feelings as with your first thought. The action that follows will be more positive in that you are likely to get in touch with the person to make sure that they are OK.

And so, the same situation has led to two very different results, depending on how you thought about the situation. How you think has affected how you felt and what you did. With the unhelpful thought you've jumped to a conclusion without very much evidence for it. This matters because it has led to a number of uncomfortable feelings and has resulted in unhelpful behaviour.

If you go home feeling depressed, you'll probably brood on what has happened and feel worse. If you get in touch with the other person, there's a good chance you'll feel better about yourself. If you don't, you won't have the chance to correct any misunderstandings about what they think of you and you will probably feel worse. This is a simplified way of looking at what happens. The whole sequence and parts of it can also feed back like this:

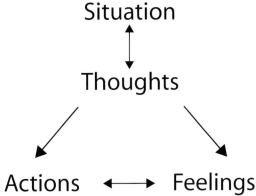

This 'vicious circle' can make you feel worse. It can even create new situations that make you feel worse. You can start to believe quite unrealistic (and unpleasant) things about yourself. This happens because when we are distressed we are more likely to jump to conclusions and to interpret things in extreme and unhelpful ways.

CBT can help you to break this vicious circle of altered thinking, feelings and behaviour. When you see the parts of the sequence clearly, you can change them and therefore change the way you feel. It aims to get you to a point where you can 'do it yourself' and work out your own ways of tackling these problems.

When CBT is applied as a cognitive behavioural management technique for children and young people in school settings in group work it looks something like this:

1. STOP
   - What is the problem situation?
   - What are your thoughts and feelings?
2. What are some of the actions/plans?
   - What can you do about the problem situation?
   - Do you need to change how you are thinking and feeling?
3. What is the best plan of action?
4. How can you do the plan?
5. Did the plan work?

Preparing for the Programme

The group facilitator, working with a staff group that has expressed interest in or had been suggested by the senior leadership team of the school, would introduce the following activity with this group, working in threes or fours depending on size:

Discuss what gains you think are reasonable to expect, after students attend a ten week anger management training programme?'

The responses should be recorded and any themes or patterns identified. The themes generated might include some of the following examples:

- Children feel better and more positive about themselves.
- Children solve conflicts for themselves.
- Improved children's awareness of the consequences of their behaviour for themselves and others.
- Children take greater responsibility for their own actions.
- Children feel empowered to talk about sensitive issues.

The facilitator would then ask the same small groups to note any implications for trainers/the school/significant others as a result of these expectations.

Based on the above the facilitator would ask the group to suggest who should run the group work programme. The paragraphs that follow outline my thinking in these areas and details how an anger management programme should be delivered.

Choosing the Staff

It is best that teachers who are respected by the children and young people selected for the programme deliver the anger management sessions. Teaching anger management skills involves the same planning and delivery elements as teaching any other academic lesson. If learning mentors and teaching assistants want to deliver the programme then steps should be taken to ensure that they are supported and/or trained by a qualified teacher. Team teaching is of course an option, although more commonly it is a teacher and learning mentor or teaching assistant that deliver the programme together.

Choosing the Pupils

In general, young people whose inappropriate behaviour is often associated with anger within the school context on a regular enough basis for there to be cause for concern would benefit most from such a programme. And children and young people who appear to 'under react' to difficult situations, for example, they may withdraw from offers of help and friendship, they may present as unforthcoming, they may seem somewhat 'depressed' by events surrounding the situation. Below are some helpful questions for school staff leading or co-ordinating a group work programme:

Appropriate identification of children and young people:

- Do these children and young people have a problem with their anger?
- Is anger management going to be the only thing the group work will cover or are their additional needs that need to be met?
- To what extent will the suggested programme in this chapter be followed exactly as it is set and to what extent will the programme be adapted or modified?

Referral mechanisms:

- Should only children and young people at school action plus be referred following review of their Individual Education Plan (IEP) showing that in-class strategies have failed to bring about the required change in behaviour?
- Is a referral form required? If so, what information should be included on the form?
- Should there be some baseline/pre-intervention (assessment) data together with post-intervention data to measure impact?
- Can children and young people refer themselves?
- Do parents/carers need to give their consent?

Staff Training

Before the actual programme begins it is recommended that all school staff teaching the young people who will be participating in the group work programme are included in a training session. There is an argument for widening the staff group training as the young people are likely to come into contact with many staff around the school and not just those who teach them. However, there are of course practical and logistical factors to be considered with whole staff training especially in larger schools.

The staff training would usually take the form of a brief outline of the theoretical basis underpinning anger management groups – the introduction to this chapter as well as the key points from the preceding three chapters.

It is also preferable that staff coming to run this group work programme have some previous experience in the art of group work. It is suggested that the process begins by bonding the group of young people together. Using activities such as those from 'Creating a Dynamic Classroom' (Hymans, 2004) are particularly helpful in this respect – especially material from the first five lessons (which cover the 'orientation' stage of group development).

Pre-Programme Measures

There are three types of pre-programme measures that are used to describe children and young people's behaviour:

1. Behaviour Checklist for staff to complete about children and young people.

2. A 'My Hot Spots' questionnaire for the children and young people to complete.

3. A Strengths and Difficulties Questionnaire (SDQ) for both staff and young people to complete.

The Behaviour Checklist and the 'My Hot Spots' questionnaire should be used in combination. The Behaviour Checklist (page 94) can also act as a screening tool for selecting pupils for the programme and the 'My Hot Spots' questionnaire (page 96) makes use of some of the ideas explored in the anger management programme.

Alternatively the SDQ can be used as the sole measure as it contains both staff and young people's ratings. The SDQ also has the advantage of being a commercial standardised questionnaire. The other advantage is that it has a 'pro-social' measure of behaviour and therefore is not simply measuring inappropriate behaviours. So if the SDQ is going to be used on its own, then the staff version should also be used as a screening tool. That means that only young people with the highest ratings should be selected for the programme.

In a primary school the above staff measures of children's behaviour are likely to be completed by the class teacher. In a secondary school staff measures about pupils' behaviour could be collected from all staff who teach the pupils, including pastoral staff such as form tutors and heads of year.

The Strengths and Difficulties Questionnaire (SDQ) is explained on page 97 and is available on the web at www.sdqinfo.comb/b1.html.

Behaviour Checklist

The profiles for pupil referrals for anger management group work are rated by staff on three measures:

1. Interactions with staff.

2. Attitudes to other pupils.

3. Personal ways.

Pupil behaviour on each of these three measures are rated by staff using ratings from 1 (almost never occurs) to 5 (occurs almost all of the time). The purpose behind the ratings is that the higher the number for each section the more serious or severe the difficulties.

As the maximum total number for each measure equals 50 a percentage figure can be obtained by multiplying the total by two. So if a pupil obtained staff ratings totals of 30 for interactions with staff; 40 for attitudes to other pupils; and 35 for personal ways, this would mean 60% of his interactions with staff were inappropriate; that he exhibited a negative attitude to other pupils 80% of the time; and that his display of his personal ways were inappropriate 70% of the time. These scores could either be used as three individual percentages or as an average percentage of (60 + 80 + 70 divided by 3) 70%. Additionally this questionnaire highlights specific behaviours that help us with the pre- and post-calculations.

'My Hot Spots' Questionnaire

Ask pupils to list things that made them angry during the week and then to rate each of these things from 1 (a little bit angry) to 5 (so angry that I started shouting and screaming), where 3 equates to being very angry. The questionnaire then asks pupils to list things that they do to make other people angry and then to rate each of these from 1 (occurs at least once during the week) to 5 (occurs at least 10 times a day), where 3 equates to an occurrence of at least once during the day.

The behaviour checklist for staff and the 'My Hot Spots' questionnaire for children are not standardised tests and they cannot therefore be considered valid or reliable measures of behaviour. They are suggested as means of gaining some indication of pupil behaviour, from staff and pupil perspectives, as a kind of benchmark for pre- and post intervention programme.

6

Summary

The chapter has stressed the importance of pre-group planning that includes staff training and consideration of the type of pupils and staff that will be involved, and some pre- and post-intervention programme measures have been introduced.

Questions for You to Consider

- What criteria will you use for choosing staff and pupils?
- How will you organise staff training and who needs to attend?
- What pre- and post-intervention measures will you use and why?
- What rewards systems will you use?
- How will you prepare the pupils for the group ending?

Behaviour Checklist

Name of Pupil: Class/Year Group:

*Ratings

- 1 = almost never occurs
- 2 = hardly occurs
- 3 = occurs about half the time
- 4 = occurs frequently
- 5 = occurs almost all of the time

1. Interactions with Staff

Behaviour	Rating*
Addresses staff noisily.	
Argues with staff at any opportunity.	
Indifferent to compliments from staff.	
Is not bothered by threat of sanctions from staff.	
Does not care whether or not staff comment on his work.	
Does not try to form any sort of relationship with staff, either good or bad.	
Messes about when staff are involved with other pupils.	
Openly behaves in ways he knows are wrong in front of staff.	
Lies without compunction.	
Regards any form of adult authority as unfair.	
Total	

2. Attitudes to Other Pupils

Behaviour	Rating*
Does not collaborate with other pupils when not able to get his own way.	
Inclined to mess about when working with other pupils.	
Disturbs other pupils and/or stops them from completing their work.	
Not able to maintain friendships with other pupils.	
Tries to show off or dominate peers in order to make friends with other pupils.	
Argues with peers and makes insulting remarks about them.	
Verbally hurtful towards the more vulnerable pupils in a group.	
Tells tales on other pupils in order to get in staff's good books.	
LViciously physically assaults other pupils.	
Is at the centre of any commotion among pupils.	
Total	

3. Personal Ways

Behaviour	Rating*
Frequently absent and known to truant.	
Loses or forgets to bring books or equipment to school.	
Destructive and damages personal belongings.	
Constantly restless in class (taps pen/pencil or ruler; jiggles with legs).	
Borrows other pupils' belongings without asking their permission.	
Grabs things from other pupils in an aggressive manner.	
Has stolen property from staff or pupils in a devious way.	
Uses foul language which he knows will gain staff disapproval.	
Has damaged school property without any acknowledgement of the consequences.	
Storms out of class when things are going against him.	
Total	

Completed by:

Designation:

Chapter 6

My Hot Spots

Name of Pupil: Class/Year Group:

1. Things that have made me angry this week:

	Rating*

*Ratings

1 = a little bit angry.

2 = quite angry.

3 = very angry.

4 = extremely angry.

5 = so angry that I was shouting and screaming.

2. Things I did to make other people angry this week:

	Rating*

*Ratings

1 = occurs at least once during the week.

2 = occurs at least three times during the week.

3 = occurs at least once a day.

4 = occurs at least 5 times a day.

5 = occurs at least 10 times a day.

The Strengths and Difficulties Questionnaire (SDQ)

The SDQ contains about 25 attributes, some positive and others negative, divided between five scales with five items in each:

1. Emotional symptoms.

2. Conduct problems.

3. Hyperactivity/inattention.

4. Peer relationship problems.

5. Pro-social behaviour.

The webpage www.sdqinfo.com/b1.html provides the following tabs which, when clicked, enable free information and downloads for general usage (there are no copyright infringements):

- What is it?

- Questionnaires, scoring instructions, scoring transparencies and record sheets to view and download.

- Scoring the SDQ.

- Uses.

- SDQ versus other questionnaires.

- Articles.

- Norms.

Chapter 7: Implementing an Anger Management Group Intervention Programme

How to Deliver the Programme

The optimal group size for the programme that follows would be six to eight young people with one teacher, although it would be helpful for the teacher and the young people to have the support of a second staff member (say a learning mentor or teaching assistant).

Incentives and rewards are also an essential part of programme delivery. Incentives could be intrinsic or extrinsic.

Intrinsic rewards should be fundamental and genuine and they will include:

- regular praise
- thanking group members for their participation
- celebrating successes
- informing parents/carers of the young people's successes.

Extrinsic incentives can include:

- orange juice, biscuits or fruit
- certificates
- trips out.

One problem with extrinsic incentives is the need to guard against possible pupil de-motivation. Pupils may say, for example, 'I don't care, take my points away,' or 'I deserve more than him.'

Each lesson should last approximately one hour and follow a varied structure of activities. However, there is usually an introductory warm-up type of activity and closing activity that looks towards positives about the session and the pupils themselves. Each lesson identifies the materials and resources required and some lessons will have materials provided at the end. The first three sessions are a very gentle introduction to anger management training with the main focus being to develop trust and group bonding. The content of these sessions is very similar to the first five lessons in Creating a Dynamic Classroom (Hymans, 2004) entitled 'Getting Acquainted'. Then sessions four to eight are described followed by the last two sessions which should ideally take place some four to six weeks after session eight. Session ten can also be run as a series of short 10-15 minute sessions. The overall aim is for the whole of the group intervention programme to be completed within a term.

7

Session One

Materials and Resources

Flipchart paper.

Pen.

A range of books (fiction and non-fiction).

Blindfolds.

Set of 'feelings' cards.

1. Introduction to the Group

The introduction to the group should be an honest but gentle account of why the young people are there. They can be told that we all find things difficult: 'I'm useless at computer games,'; 'My daughter can't ride a bike,'; 'You have trouble with your temper.' The introduction might then continue along the lines of: 'This is no big deal, let's get down and teach you how to get your temper under control.' It is usually helpful to go round the group to see if any members want to stay as they are – it is unusual for anyone to say they do. This is because what is being offered to the young people comes as a great relief. They know full well that things are not right but they do not see a way out of their current situation. The group work programme offers them a way out of a hole as well as giving them permission to stop digging!

2. Ground Rules

Most group work practitioners start groups with a discussion about ground rules. This is best done if all group members agree that rules are needed and the members generate the rules. A helpful starting point is to ask the group why we have rules in general. Teachers can offer the following if there is no response from group members or as a means of summarising how the group responded:

- Some rules are made to prevent confusion, for example, the rule that cars must drive on one side of the road (reference can be made to which side of the road this is for cars in the UK and the likely confusion if there was a switch or when right hand drive cars are taken abroad).

- Some rules are made to be enjoyed, for example, the rules of football and netball are an important part in making these games enjoyable for both players and spectators.

- Some rules are made by organisations for their own members, for example, the rule that children and young people must wear a particular type of uniform at school.

- Some rules are made to prevent a few people from taking advantage of everyone else, for example, the rule that you must not steal.

- In general, the purpose of a rule is to make life easier and better for the majority of people.

The types of ground rules elicited from group members often include the following:

- We agree to take turns.
- Only one person to talk at one time.
- No putdowns.
- I can talk to other young people about what I did in the group but not what my friends in the group did.
- We agree to be on time.

3. Ice Breaker

The students are divided into pairs and asked to list three things that they have in common with each other. They can be prompted by suggesting the football team they support; the type of music they listen to; the TV programmes they watch. Each pair then takes turns to share one thing with the larger group until all the things listed have been covered. The complete list can be recorded on a flipchart by the teacher.

4. My Favourite Page

Tell the children that they have three minutes to choose a book that they think looks interesting to them. Encourage the children to choose a number of books as they go along and then choose the best two or three at the thirty second warning, then the best one at the ten second warning. The children are then given two minutes to choose the best page in their book. Again encourage them to choose a number of pages as they go along and choose the best two or three at the twenty second warning and the best page at the ten second warning. You then give the children one minute to choose the best thing on the page they have chosen. Give them a warning about ten seconds before time is up. Then give the children thirty seconds to say what it is about the page in the book that they found interesting.

When the children are telling about their page they should make eye contact with the rest of the group and speak clearly and confidently. This is really an assertiveness game. The listeners should be assertive in their listening, nodding and making eye contact.

7

5. Walking Blindfold

This involves the children working in pairs. One is blindfolded, while the other leads their partner around the room. The leader holds the blindfolded pupil gently by the elbow and helps steer them as well as delivering a string of instructions and information about where they are, what is coming next and what is about to happen. This game helps to develop trust.

6. The Last Time I Felt

To play this game you will need a set of 'Feeling Cards' with the children seated in a circle. If you have non-readers, get the children to hold their cards toward the centre of the group. You can then give them the word by saying, 'Josh would you tell us when you last felt angry (or whatever is written on their card).' Begin this game by modelling it, 'The last time I felt sad was when I broke a vase that my mother had given me as a special present,' and pass the sad card to someone else in the group. The sad card is then passed around the group. Then you take a second 'feeling card', give it to a child and ask him to start the game by saying, for example: 'The last time I felt happy was when...' The number of feeling cards you are able to use will be very much dependent upon how much time you have remaining for the session given that there is one final, albeit much shorter, activity remaining. 'The last time I felt' is also repeated in Session Three.

7. Positives about the Session

With the children in a circle, begin by saying one positive thing about the group session. For instance, 'I really enjoyed the way the group collaborated with each other today.' Ask a child on your right to say something positive about the session. This is continued going round the circle.

Feelings Cards

Sad	Hurt
Angry	Bored
Happy	Silly
Upset	Stupid
Frightened	Cross

Feelings Cards

Gutted	Clever
Scared	Keen
Confused	Excited
Embarassed	Proud
Lonely	Humiliated

Session Two

Materials and Resources

Flipchart paper.

Pen.

1. Check In

This is a simple but essential component of any group that seeks to be supportive. Each member of the group takes their turn to report on their week. Instigate this by asking an age appropriate question such as, 'Has anybody got any news?' or 'How have things been?' With an anger management group this will become the core component of the group's work. This is the time when the children will tell you about the difficult situations they have been in during the week. If they don't you will no doubt be aware from your own observations or from other staff that there have been some difficulties. You can bring these up if the child doesn't. The way I tackle the problems that are discussed is to give the group a summary of the child's account of the event and ask if anyone can suggest how this situation could have been handled. The whole group is then immersed in a sea of words that will encourage the development of a more complex array of strategies for coping with situations. You may need to note down the alternative options and then one by one ask the group to predict the outcome of each alternative, in its fullest sense. For instance, 'What would be likely to happen if John told the teacher that Tom had spat at him?' 'Tom would get in trouble,' 'John would be allowed to go to the toilet and clean himself up.'

2. What We Could Do if…

This game is similar to the exploration of difficulties experienced by the children and detailed in 'Check In'. The only difference being that you offer the children hypothetical situations. For instance, what could you do if a:
- boy hits you in the playground
- girl pulls your hair in assembly
- ball is deliberately thrown at you in the playground?

Again note down the different options offered by the group. Explore the consequences for each option to the fullest extent, using a sentence like, 'What would happen if you did that?'

3. I Catch You and You Catch me

This is a trust game. Meaning that you must trust the children to play it responsibly and the children must trust each other, which they do in turn. Put the children in pairs of approximately equal physical stature. Demonstrate the game by standing behind a volunteer, with your hands poised just behind her shoulders. Then ask the volunteer to keep their legs stiff and fall backwards. As they fall back you push them forwards again.

Gradually increase the amount the children fall. It feels absolutely wonderful, particularly if you close you eyes.

4. Positive About the Person on Your Left

Put the children in a circle and model saying a positive comment to the person on your left, for example, 'Jamail, I really like your hair,' and then smile. Ask the children to do the same. They may find this difficult and need lots of encouragement.

5. Positive About Yourself

Keep the children in a circle and begin by saying something positive about yourself. Maintain eye contact with the group whilst you are doing it. For instance, 'I like myself because I try to be happy all the time.' Then ask a child on your left or right to say something positive about themselves. At first the children will probably say something about liking their trainers. Let this go at first but slowly and gently push for something about them as people. Saying something like: 'Yes, I like your trainers too, but try to think of something you like about your personality, not about something that you are wearing.' If you have a child that is reluctant the following approach is sometimes useful, say something like, 'Tyreka is having trouble with this one, lets help her out and all say something positive about her.'

This will immerse Tyreka in a sea of positive language about herself and give her some ideas. If this still fails, pick two of the positives that she has heard from the group and offer a choice. Something like, 'OK Tyreka you have nice hair and a great smile which one do you want to say?' If that doesn't work leave the child for that week. They will think about it before the next group and say something next time the group meets.

6. Positives about the Session

With the children in a circle, begin by saying one positive thing about the group session. For instance, 'I really enjoyed the way the group collaborated with each other today.' Ask a child on your right to say something positive about the session. This is continued going round the circle.

Session Three

Pre-Preparation

Prior to this session, the facilitator will need to have explained to the group the difference between the following:

- Submissive (or passive) – that is, giving in without objection or resistance.
- Assertive – that is, confident, positive and insistent.
- Aggressive – that is, inclined to act in an angry or hostile manner.

Alternatively the facilitator will need to explain these roles prior to beginning the activity, 'Taking a Book Back to a Shop'.

Materials and Resources

Feeling cards.

Flipchart paper.

Pen.

Book.

1. Check In

This is a simple but essential component of any group that seeks to be supportive. Each member of the group takes their turn to report on their week. Instigate this by asking an age appropriate question such as, 'Has anybody got any news?' or 'How have things been?' With an anger management group this will become the core component of the group's work. This is the time when the children will tell you about the difficult situations they have been in during the week. If they don't you will no doubt be aware from your own observations or from other staff that there have been some difficulties. You can bring these up if the child doesn't. The way I tackle the problems that are discussed is to give the group a summary of the child's account of the event and ask if anyone can suggest how this situation could have been handled. The whole group is then immersed in a sea of words that will encourage the development of a more complex array of strategies for coping with situations. You may need to note down the alternative options and then one by one ask the group to predict the outcome of each alternative, in its fullest sense. For instance, 'What would be likely to happen if John told the teacher that Tom had spat at him?' 'Tom would get in trouble,' 'John would be allowed to go to the toilet and clean himself up.'

2. The Last Time I Felt

To play this game you will need a set of 'Feeling Cards' with the children seated in a circle. If you have non-readers, get the children to hold their cards toward the centre of the group. You can then give them the word by saying, 'Josh would you tell us when you last felt angry (or whatever is written on their card).' Begin this game by modelling it: 'The last time I felt sad was when I broke a vase that my mother had given me as a special present,' and pass the sad card to someone else in the group. The sad card is then passed around the group. Then you take a second 'feeling card', give it to a child and ask him to start the game by saying, 'The last time I felt happy was when…' The number of feeling cards you are able to use will be very much dependent upon how much time you have remaining for the session given that there is one final, albeit much shorter, activity remaining.

3. Taking a Book Back to a Shop

This is an assertiveness game. The scenario is that a book has been purchased from a shop and it has a page missing. The children take it in turns to be the customer taking the book back and to be the shopkeeper. There are three roles for the customer. Mr Wimp (submissive), Mr Angry (aggressive) and Mr Strong (assertive). It is usually a good idea to let the children try Wimp and Angry and only model if they don't get it right. The teacher should always model Strong. After each role-play ask the shopkeeper how he felt, ask the customer how he felt and ask the children who observed how they felt. Usually Mr Wimp makes everybody feel like they don't want to change the book, whilst Mr Angry gets everybody cross. The strong approach means that the customer comes away from the shop with a new book. Because, by being assertive, people want to help you. The important lesson here is the effect being angry has on other people and that there is a much better way.

4. Positive About the Person on Your Left

Put the children in a circle and model saying a positive comment to the person on your left, for example, 'Jamail, I really like your hair,' and then smile. Ask the children to do the same. They may find this difficult and need lots of encouragement.

5. Positive About Yourself

Keep the children in a circle and begin by saying something positive about yourself. Maintain eye contact with the group whilst you are doing it. For instance, 'I like myself because I try to be happy all the time.' Then ask a child on your left or right to say something positive about themselves. At first the children will probably say something about liking their trainers. Let this go at first but slowly and gently push for something about them as people. Saying something like: 'Yes, I like your trainers too, but try to think of something you like about your personality, not about something that you are wearing.' If you have a child that is reluctant the following approach is sometimes useful, say something like, 'Tyreka is having trouble with this one, lets help her out and all say something positive about her.'

This will immerse Tyreka in a sea of positive language about herself and give her some ideas. If this still fails, pick two of the positives that she has heard from the group and offer a choice. Something like, 'OK Tyreka you have nice hair and a great smile which one do you want to say?' If that doesn't work leave the child for that week. They will think about it before the next group and say something next time the group meets.

6. Relaxation

This is a very simple but powerful technique that can be used to good effect with children as young as six, but is probably more effective with older children. The idea is to tense each part of the body, note the feeling of tension and tightness and then relax and go floppy. After about one month of regular practice a stimulus is needed. With adults a red dot is ordinarily put onto their watch and upon seeing the dot they will check their body for tension. With older children the watch technique can and does work. With younger children they may need some form of mark on the board or perhaps a soft toy placed where they might tend to look regularly. The children would usually be sitting in a chair although I have found that some children rather like to practice this laying on beanbags. This is a helpful form of words to use:

'Sit comfortably close your eyes and think of nothing.

Now make your hands into fists, go on really squeeze those fists. Feel that tight feeling. Feel that tight feeling and now relax and go floppy. Think of that lovely feeling of relaxation (or think of that lovely floppy feeling for younger children). Make your hands into tight fists again and bring your hands up to touch your shoulders. Feel that tight feeling along your arms. Feel the tight feeling and relax, think of that lovely feeling of relaxation (or think of that lovely floppy feeling).

Now relax your arms, let them hang loosely by your side. Push your shoulders up and try and touch your ears. Go on really push upwards. Feel that tight feeling in your shoulders. Feel the tight feeling and relax, think of that lovely feeling of relaxation (lovely floppy feeling).

This time scrunch up your face. Really scrunch up your face. Feel that tight feeling in your face and relax, think of that lovely feeling of relaxation (lovely floppy feeling).

Now make your stomach (tummy) muscles tight. Go on, really tighten those muscles. Feel that tight feeling. Feel the tight feeling and relax, think of that lovely feeling of relaxation (lovely floppy feeling).

Push your stomach (tummy) forward this time, make your back arch, feel the tight feeling all along your back. Feel that tight feeling and relax, think of that wonderful feeling of relaxation.

Tighten the muscles in your legs, feel those muscles tightening, feel that tight feeling and relax. Feel that tight feeling along your arms. Feel the tight feeling and relax, think of that lovely feeling of relaxation (lovely floppy feeling).

Now curl your toes into a tight ball, really scrunch up those toes. Feel that tight feeling. Feel the tight feeling and relax, think of that lovely feeling of relaxation (lovely floppy feeling.)

Take a deep breath. Hold that breath, feel that tight feeling in your lungs. Feel the tight feeling then let the breath out slowly and feel all the tightness go away. Think of that lovely feeling of relaxation (lovely floppy feeling).

Keep your eyes closed. We are going to check each part of your body to see if there is any tightness. Think of your hands and arms. If there is any tightness just let go of it. Now check your shoulders neck and face. If you find any tightness just let go. Check your back and shoulders, your legs and feet. If you find any tension just let go. You should now be feeling wonderful and relaxed/floppy. Just enjoy that wonderful feeling and when you feel ready, open your eyes.'

7

7. Positives about the Session

With the children in a circle, begin by saying one positive thing about the group session. For instance, 'I really enjoyed the way the group collaborated with each other today.' Ask a child on your right to say something positive about the session. This is continued going round the circle.

Session Four

This is where the anger management training begins as we begin to unpack the cues that children feel warrant an angry response.

Materials and Resources

Flipchart paper.

Pen.

Blindfold.

Variety of objects for the 'Pick a Trust Game'.

'The Interview' activity page.

A rubbish bin (optional).

1. Check in

This is a simple but essential component of any group that seeks to be supportive. Each member of the group takes their turn to report on their week. Instigate this by asking an age appropriate question such as, 'Has anybody got any news?' or 'How have things been?' With an anger management group this will become the core component of the group's work. This is the time when the children will tell you about the difficult situations they have been in during the week. If they don't you will no doubt be aware from your own observations or from other staff that there have been some difficulties. You can bring these up if the child doesn't. The way I tackle the problems that are discussed is to give the group a summary of the child's account of the event and ask if anyone can suggest how this situation could have been handled. The whole group is then immersed in a sea of words that will encourage the development of a more complex array of strategies for coping with situations. You may need to note down the alternative options and then one by one ask the group to predict the outcome of each alternative, in its fullest sense. For instance, 'What would be likely to happen if John told the teacher that Tom had spat at him?' 'Tom would get in trouble,' 'John would be allowed to go to the toilet and clean himself up.'

2. Pick a Trust Game

(i) Have a group member stand in the centre of the room and blindfold them. Everyone else moves around until the blindfolded group member says, 'Still Pond.' He then moves forward and explores a face and guesses who it is. If the guess is right, the volunteer takes off the blindfold; if not, he tries again. For a variation, as he moves forward, people can make music or noises while he searches for a specific person. (For example, 'I'm going to find David.')

(ii) Emphasise that this is a non-verbal, non-visual experience, using one's other senses. Ask group members to choose a partner that they would like to know better. In each pair, one member, 'A', closes her eyes (or is blindfolded). They can communicate with each other only through touch. The second member of each pair, 'B', leads and helps 'A' to experience the world around through her other senses. B is to protect the partner, show her how gentle he can be and try to give her a truly pleasant experience. After five minutes, ask 'A' and 'B' to switch roles. Ask each pair to discuss their experiences by themselves and then ask them to feed back their discussion to the whole group.

(iii) Objects are scattered in an indoor or outdoor place. In pairs, one person verbally guides her blindfolded partner through the minefield.

(iv) In pairs of similar size, one becomes a Faller and one the Catcher. Show children how to spot when someone is about to fall and when and how to catch. Start small and build to bigger falls, then swap. Debrief and ask, 'What made you feel more or less trusting?'

(v) In pairs, one person is blindfolded. Holding hands, the blindfolded person is lead gradually from a slow walk up to fast running. Swap.

3. The Interview

The activity page, 'The Interview', covers six areas:

1. What sorts of things do people get angry about at school?
2. How can you tell by just looking at someone that they are starting to feel angry inside?
3. How could you help a friend who was feeling angry about something?
4. How do you keep your cool in difficult situations?
5. What might the consequences be if you lost your temper with a friend?
6. What might the consequences be if you lost your temper with a member of staff at school?

Divide the group into threes, and ask each member of the threesome to take on one role, that is, being the interviewer, being interviewed and recording the interview. At the end of the interviews, a summary of the notes taken by the students should be recorded on a flipchart and they can be discussed, especially in terms of the similarities and differences between the pupils in each of the six areas. Note that the answers to question one, 'At school what sorts of things do people get angry about?' are used in the next activity.

4. In the Bin

For this activity the children need to be seated in a circle. You can if you wish place a real bin in the middle, but an imaginary one is usually best. Bring out your list of things that make the children angry from the first question in 'The Interview' and select one that refers to name-calling. Ask them to call you that name. If for instance being told, 'Your mum is ugly,' particularly offends Jacob then ask Jacob to say it to you. You will find that the children find this very difficult. It is very important that the children and the facilitator have bonded before playing this game as it does take the children close to the edge of being very angry at first. So if you find the children are not in the least reticent about calling you names you might like to consider if the group is ready for this activity.

Once you have persuaded Jacob to tell you that your mum is ugly, respond by talking the phrase out. For instance, 'You don't know my mum so you can't know. My mum is not ugly she is a very nice person and I love her. What you're saying is a load of rubbish, in the bin!' Deliver this with hand gestures to symbolise screwing up rubbish and throwing it into the bin.

You may need to model this a few times until you feel the children are ready for their go. Ask for a volunteer. Remind the children that this activity is designed to help them deal with comments in a way that does not make them upset. If you are sure that the child will just about hold in there, then say to Jacob, 'Your mum is ugly.' Gently encourage Josh to talk the insult out and toss it in the bin. Once he has, clap, shake hands and say well done, the child must be made to feel secure, loved and happy.

You will need to get the children familiar with talking out insults from the facilitator before taking the next step which is to allow the children to insult each other. Once you have got them to this level the children will have come a very long way.

5. I Feel Great When

This is a wind down game to encourage positive thinking. The children might start with saying they feel great when their favourite football team scores a goal. If they do, make your response a model to follow. For instance, 'I feel great when someone is rude to me in a supermarket and I keep my temper.' The essence is to get the children to say they feel great when they have done something rather than when something is done to them, such as someone else scoring a goal or there is a good show on television.

6. Positives about the Session

With the children in a circle, begin by saying one positive thing about the group session. For instance, 'I really enjoyed the way the group collaborated with each other today.' Ask a child on your right to say something positive about the session. This is continued going round the circle.

7

The Interview

1. What sorts of things do people get angry about at school?

2. How can you tell by just looking at someone that they are starting to feel angry inside?

3. How could you help a friend who was feeling angry about something?

4. How do you keep your cool in difficult situations?

5. What might the consequences be if you lost your temper with a friend?

6. What might the consequences be if you lost your temper with a member of staff at school?

Session Five

Flipchart paper or notepad.

Pen.

1. Check In

This is a simple but essential component of any group that seeks to be supportive. Each member of the group takes their turn to report on their week. Instigate this by asking an age appropriate question such as, 'Has anybody got any news?' or 'How have things been?' With an anger management group this will become the core component of the group's work. This is the time when the children will tell you about the difficult situations they have been in during the week. If they don't you will no doubt be aware from your own observations or from other staff that there have been some difficulties. You can bring these up if the child doesn't. The way I tackle the problems that are discussed is to give the group a summary of the child's account of the event and ask if anyone can suggest how this situation could have been handled. The whole group is then immersed in a sea of words that will encourage the development of a more complex array of strategies for coping with situations. You may need to note down the alternative options and then one by one ask the group to predict the outcome of each alternative, in its fullest sense. For instance, 'What would be likely to happen if John told the teacher that Tom had spat at him?' 'Tom would get in trouble,' 'John would be allowed to go to the toilet and clean himself up.'

2. I Made a Good Choice

This game reinforces 'The Interview' and gives the children the opportunity to receive acclaim for being in a difficult situation and making a good choice. Try to get the children to detail the range of choices they had available to them. A typical interaction between the child, facilitator and group might go like this:

Child:	The time I made a choice was last week when John came up to me in class and whispered, 'Your mum raids bins for your dinner.' I just sat there.
Facilitator:	How did you feel?
Child:	I felt angry and wanted to get up and hit him.
Facilitator:	What choices did you have?
Child:	Tell the teacher or ignore him.
Facilitator (to group):	Did (target child) have any other choices?
Member of group:	He could have hit him or shouted at him.
Facilitator (to group):	Seems like (target child) made a great choice. Let's all shake his hand and say well done.

You can extend this activity by getting the children in the group or the target child to predict what the consequences would have been had they chosen any of the other options. This may seem a little long-winded, but as the pupils get into the swing of this they become very adept at it, which is what you are aiming at. The children should be able to think very quickly about what will happen if they make a choice and thus begin to make the choices that are in their best interests, and keep them out of trouble.

3. Ten Nasty Things that Other People Might Do to Me

This game is linked inextricably to 'Sort in Order' (Activity 4 below) and 'Responses to the Ten Nasty Things that Other People Might Do to Me' (Session Six).

Have a notepad on your knee or use a flipchart. Ask the children to tell you some nasty things that other people might do to them. You need a range from ignore to attack physically (for example, ignore me, tell lies about me, cuss my mum, slap me, punch me).

The key question to use here is something like, 'That's an excellent example. Can you tell me something that is worse or something that is not so bad?' In this way you will get a range. Write each one as a discreet unit with a line between it and the next nasty thing on your pad or flipchart.

4. Sort in Order the Nasty Things that Other People Might Do to Me

Cut each of the 'nasty things' into a separate slip of paper.

Place the children around a table with the slips on the table and ask them to put the most offensive nasty thing at the top and the least offensive at the bottom. The key question here would be something along the lines of, 'Do you think that someone being rude about your mum is worse than being slapped or being punched?'

In this way by working down the hierarchy that the children have produced they will have given thought to offences against them and will begin to see that some are worse than others. This process helps the children to become more complex cognitively.

Once there is agreement, the most offensive nasty thing is then numbered 'ten' and the least offensive nasty thing is numbered 'one' by the group leader. This numbered list will need to be kept for Sessions Six and Seven.

5. Positive about Someone I Dislike

This is a real tough one for the children because they have become used to actively disliking some people, and when one of those people gives offence in some way they retaliate for the original offence with an additional element that is there because they dislike the offender. This to an outside observer would be seen as an overreaction on the part of our target child. Naturally, the target child feels they have responded fairly which they probably have on their scale of things, hence the disbelief at the consequences that follow and a feeling that they have been unfairly treated.

It is therefore very important to get this game off the ground. It may take some time to get each child to get to the point where they can do this, just be patient. The person who is disliked should not be mentioned by name, a model response would be, 'The person I dislike has a good sense of humour.'

6. The Last Time I was Kind

Another wind down game but similarly one that requires a degree of risk for a child, that is, used to keeping others at a distance. With the children in a circle begin by modeling, 'The last time I was kind, I gave my next door neighbour a hand to change the tyre on his car when it had a puncture.' Ask a child on your left or right to continue. If you wish, you can extend this with two questions, 'How did they feel?' and 'How did you feel?' You can also allow the group to ask questions.

7. Positives about the Session

With the children in a circle, begin by saying one positive thing about the group session. For instance, 'I really enjoyed the way the group collaborated with each other today.' Ask a child on your right to say something positive about the session. This is continued going round the circle.

7

Session Six

Materials and Resources

Flipchart paper.

Pen.

Numbered list of 'nasty things that other people might do to me'.

1. Check In

This is a simple but essential component of any group that seeks to be supportive. Each member of the group takes their turn to report on their week. Instigate this by asking an age appropriate question such as, 'Has anybody got any news?' or 'How have things been?' With an anger management group this will become the core component of the group's work. This is the time when the children will tell you about the difficult situations they have been in during the week. If they don't you will no doubt be aware from your own observations or from other staff that there have been some difficulties. You can bring these up if the child doesn't. The way I tackle the problems that are discussed is to give the group a summary of the child's account of the event and ask if anyone can suggest how this situation could have been handled. The whole group is then immersed in a sea of words that will encourage the development of a more complex array of strategies for coping with situations. You may need to note down the alternative options and then one by one ask the group to predict the outcome of each alternative, in its fullest sense. For instance, 'What would be likely to happen if John told the teacher that Tom had spat at him?' 'Tom would get in trouble,' 'John would be allowed to go to the toilet and clean himself up.'

2. I Made a Bad Choice

This is similar to 'I Made a Good Choice' (page 115). The reason you play it after the positive version is that it is important to gain the children's trust first. Once the group bonds with each other and you, the children don't want to disappoint you and so seek to put a gloss over their behaviour. The desire to please you is a vital part of the change process. But it is very important that the children recognise when they have made a mistake and are given the chance to reflect on it. So this game is more a celebration of the fact that we all make mistakes, but what is important is to recognise that mistake and fix it. An analogy can be made with spelling by explaining that you don't get spellings right first time it is only by looking at the word spelt wrong, seeing where you went wrong and then fixing it that you learn.

Present the game as described above. Ask the children to identify an incident, preferably recent, or if they are reluctant, from the past, and say what choice they made and what would have been a better choice. Get the group or the child to explore the choice and see what happened versus what would have happened if they had made a better choice. Record the children's response on a flipchart.

3. Things that I Might Do in Response to the Nasty Things that Other People Might Do to Me

This is an identical process to that described in 'Ten Nasty Things that Other People Might Do to Me' (page 116). Have a notepad on your knee or use a flipchart and show the children the numbered list of nasty things that other people might do to them from Activity 4 in Session Five to act as a stimulus. It would be best if this list was on a flipchart so all the children could see it.

Ask the children to give you some possible ways of responding to these nasty things in general without specifying which responses were related to which of the nasty things on the list. You would need a range that might include: ignore or walk, tell the teacher, cuss, slap or push over.

Here, the key question would be something along the lines of, 'That's a good example, now can you tell me something that would be worse than that?' Once the list has been generated it is used for the next activity. You should write each response as a discreet unit with a line between it and the next response on your pad or the flipchart.

4. Sort in Order the Things I Might Do in Response to the Nasty Things that Other People Might Do to Me

Begin by cutting each of the responses (from Activity 3) into a separate slip of paper. Place the children around the table with the slips of paper in the centre and ask them to order the responses for any situation in general from '1' (least appropriate) to 10 (most appropriate). Here the key questions would be, for example, 'Is walking away from a situation more or less appropriate than ignoring it?' 'Is telling the teacher more or less appropriate than cussing someone?'

It has to be acknowledged that some responses may be context specific. The main purpose is to generate a hierarchical list of response from least to most appropriate.

Put the numbered strips away in a safe place as they will be needed again for session seven.

5. I Shared

This is simply a wind down game but it does require a degree of courage for a child that is quite self-protective and self-contained to admit to having been generous to another. With the children sitting in a circle, begin this game by modelling. 'The last time I can remember sharing was on Sunday when I bought a bar of chocolate to share with my daughter.' Ask a child on your right to continue.

6. Positives about the Session

With the children in a circle, begin by saying one positive thing about the group session. For instance, 'I really enjoyed the way the group collaborated with each other today.' Ask a child on your right to say something positive about the session. This is continued going round the circle.

Session Seven

Materials and Resources

Flipchart.

Pen.

Numbered list of the nasty things that other people might do to me.

Numbered list of the things I might do in response to the nasty things that other people might do to me.

1. Check In

This is a simple but essential component of any group that seeks to be supportive. Each member of the group takes their turn to report on their week. Instigate this by asking an age appropriate question such as, 'Has anybody got any news?' or 'How have things been?' With an anger management group this will become the core component of the group's work. This is the time when the children will tell you about the difficult situations they have been in during the week. If they don't you will no doubt be aware from your own observations or from other staff that there have been some difficulties. You can bring these up if the child doesn't. The way I tackle the problems that are discussed is to give the group a summary of the child's account of the event and ask if anyone can suggest how this situation could have been handled. The whole group is then immersed in a sea of words that will encourage the development of a more complex array of strategies for coping with situations. You may need to note down the alternative options and then one by one ask the group to predict the outcome of each alternative, in its fullest sense. For instance, 'What would be likely to happen if John told the teacher that Tom had spat at him?' 'Tom would get in trouble,' 'John would be allowed to go to the toilet and clean himself up.'

2. I Shared

This is simply a wind down game but it does require a degree of courage for a child that is quite self-protective and self-contained to admit to having been generous to another. With the children sitting in a circle, begin this game by modelling. 'The last time I can remember sharing was on Sunday when I bought a bar of chocolate to share with my daughter.' Ask a child on your right to continue.

3. What I Would Do If…

For this session you will need your carefully preserved slips with numbered lists of the nasty things that other people might do to me and the numbered list of the things I might do in response.

Seat the children around a table and lay out the two sets of lists. Select at random one of the nasty things that other people might do to me from the list, for example, 'cuss my mum' (which might have been numbered as five out of ten where one is the least offensive and ten is the most offensive). Then ask the children to look at the list of 'things I might do in response' and ask them to place a fair response next to it. The clue is that the children should be picking a response that is also numbered around five (which might be, for example, 'tell them to stop and say why'). If you get a response, for example, 'slap them', which may be numbered two out of a possible ten response, you can point this out and see if the children want to reconsider their response.

On the other hand you might get an almost equally high-numbered response of say ten out of a possible ten (that is, 'punch them') to a high-numbered nasty thing, say nine (that is, 'spits at me'). You will then need to discuss with the children the possible consequences of matching the numbers when the nasty thing is highly offensive. You can also discuss with the children the possibility of making more than one response, especially in the light of a more offensive nasty thing happening to them. So, for example, the nasty thing might be 'kicks me' (numbered ten out of ten) and the response might be 'warn them' (numbered four) and then 'tell the teacher' (numbered three) if the child is kicked again. You can then repeat this activity by picking another numbered 'nasty thing' and ask the children to place a fair response next to it until you feel the children have had enough.

The chart on page 122 provides a helpful prompt sheet.

4. Positive about School

Another wind down game but important non the less because we want the children to feel positively about school and being immersed if briefly in a sea of positive words about school can only help this process. Begin by modeling, 'I like this school because it is a school that really cares about children who are having difficulties.' Be strict here and insist upon positives and no silly comments.

5. Firm Handshake and Farewell

Here you are seeking to develop a firm assertive handshake with eye contact. Remember many of the children in an anger management group will not have developed assertive skills. They may know how to be submissive when confronted with a much stronger adversary or how to give an aggressive hard stare. So don't be surprised if this comes a little difficult at first. Model this by holding out your hand whilst making eye contact and saying, 'Thank you for all your hard work today.' Expect the children to make eye contact with you and to maintain eye contact during the interaction and say quietly yet firmly, 'Thank you.' After a while the children get really good at this and you can do a round of hand shaking very quickly.

7

What I Would Do If...

Nasty Things

Least offensive

1.

2.

3.

4.

5.

6.

7.

8.

9.

10.

Most offensive

Responses

Least offensive

1.

2.

3.

4.

5.

6.

7.

8.

9.

10.

Most offensive

Session Eight

This session is intentionally a repeat of Session Seven as some very important cognitive re-organisation goes on during Session Seven, especially during 'What I Would Do If...' (page 122). Some very fundamental beliefs are also addressed and altered. For this reason, Session Seven can be quite demanding and so these issues are returned to in a repeat session in order to try and reinforce the underpinning cognitive re-organisation of children's thinking processes, especially when others commit offences against them. Session Eight is also the last session before the follow-up sessions that follow.

Materials and Resources

Flipchart.

Pen.

Numbered list of the nasty things that other people might do to me.

Numbered list of the things I might do in response to the nasty things that other people might do to me.

1. Check In

This is a simple but essential component of any group that seeks to be supportive. Each member of the group takes their turn to report on their week. Instigate this by asking an age appropriate question such as, 'Has anybody got any news?' or 'How have things been?' With an anger management group this will become the core component of the group's work. This is the time when the children will tell you about the difficult situations they have been in during the week. If they don't you will no doubt be aware from your own observations or from other staff that there have been some difficulties. You can bring these up if the child doesn't. The way I tackle the problems that are discussed is to give the group a summary of the child's account of the event and ask if anyone can suggest how this situation could have been handled. The whole group is then immersed in a sea of words that will encourage the development of a more complex array of strategies for coping with situations. You may need to note down the alternative options and then one by one ask the group to predict the outcome of each alternative, in its fullest sense. For instance, 'What would be likely to happen if John told the teacher that Tom had spat at him?' 'Tom would get in trouble,' 'John would be allowed to go to the toilet and clean himself up.'

2. I Shared

This is simply a wind down game but it does require a degree of courage for a child that is quite self-protective and self-contained to admit to having been generous to another. With the children sitting in a circle, begin this game by modelling. 'The last time I can remember sharing was on Sunday when I bought a bar of chocolate to share with my daughter.' Ask a child on your right to continue.

3. What I Would Do If...

For this session you will need your carefully preserved slips with numbered lists of the nasty things that other people might do to me and the numbered list of the things I might do in response.

Seat the children around a table and lay out the two sets of lists. Select at random one of the nasty things that other people might do to me from the list, for example, 'cuss my mum' (which might have been numbered as five out of ten where one is the least offensive and ten is the most offensive). Then ask the children to look at the list of 'things I might do in response' and ask them to place a fair response next to it. The clue is that the children should be picking a response that is also numbered around five (which might be, for example, 'tell them to stop and say why'). If you get a response, for example, 'slap them', which may be numbered two out of a possible ten response, you can point this out and see if the children want to reconsider their response.

On the other hand you might get an almost equally high-numbered response of say ten out of a possible ten (that is, 'punch them') to a high-numbered nasty thing say nine (that is, 'spits at me'). You will then need to discuss with the children the possible consequences of matching the numbers when the nasty thing is highly offensive. You can also discuss with the children the possibility of making more than one response, especially in the light of a more offensive nasty thing happening to them. So, for example, the nasty thing might be 'kicks me' (numbered ten out of ten) and the response might be 'warn them' (numbered four) and then 'tell the teacher' (numbered three) if the child is kicked again. You can then repeat this activity by picking another numbered 'nasty thing' and ask the children to place a fair response next to it until you feel the children have had enough.

4. Positive about School

Another wind down game but important non the less because we want the children to feel positively about school and being immersed if briefly in a sea of positive words about school can only help this process. Begin by modeling, 'I like this school because it is a school that really cares about children who are having difficulties.' Be strict here and insist upon positives and no silly comments.

5. Firm Handshake and Farewell

Here you are seeking to develop a firm assertive handshake with eye contact. Remember many of the children in an anger management group will not have developed assertive skills. They may know how to be submissive when confronted with a much stronger adversary or how to give an aggressive hard stare. So don't be surprised if this comes a little difficult at first. Model this by holding out your hand whilst making eye contact and saying, 'Thank you for all your hard work today.' Expect the children to make eye contact with you and to maintain eye contact during the interaction and say quietly yet firmly, 'Thank you.' After a while the children get really good at this and you can do a round of hand shaking very quickly.

Session Nine

Materials and Resources

Flipchart.

Pen.

Anger Management Cards.

Magnetic Noughts and Crosses game.

Snakes and Ladders games.

Chess sets.

You will need to run sessions nine and ten to support the children as they adjust their behaviour. These sessions should ideally be run a little while after Session Eight, say four to six weeks later. This may be a very uncertain time. By now you will be responding to the needs of the children when planning sessions. Make them fun but include check in, as this will enable the group to address any problems that have arisen since the group formally ended. Now is the time to let the children play board games, such as snakes and ladders or noughts and crosses. It is important that they play the board games according to your rules of social behaviour.

Sample Support Session

1. Check In

This time check in is used to check to see if any problems have arisen over the last six to eight weeks rather than over a previous week.

2. Suggestions for Managing the Problems that have Arisen

Some suggestions can be brainstormed from the group in pairs or as a whole group. Suggestions from the brainstorming activity can be made into anger management cards. Two blank cards are included with the Anger Management Cards (page 127). They can be printed from the CD-ROM onto card and laminated for the pupils to keep together with additional suggestions from the brainstorming activity in responding to new problems that have arisen from the Check In activity.

3. Board Games

It is important to be a good loser and a good winner and it is possible to develop these skills within a group context by the use of board games in three phases.

Phase one:

Use a magnetic game of Noughts and Crosses. This game is very quick thus there is little invested and so the disappointment of losing is not severe. Insist that the loser says, 'Congratulations,' to the winner. The winner has to say to the loser, 'Thank you for playing.' Be very firm here as this sets the scene for the rest of the games.

7

Phase two:

Snakes and ladders. This game has more investment than Noughts and Crosses. It is very useful because it has lots of disappointments and moments of elation. It is important that the moments of disappointment are not jeered at by the others, nor that the moments of elation are a chance to sneer at the opponents. Insist on the following behaviours: upon having to go down a snake, the group say, 'Hard luck,' and the target child says, 'Thank you.' Reinforce this by asking how they feel when people show sympathy and by asking the group how they feel when showing sympathy as compared to sneering. Again the winner says, 'Thank you,' for playing and the losers say, 'Congratulations.'

Phase three:

Chess. You may need to spend some time teaching the children to play chess in a one-to-one. However, this is a game that has a very great deal of investment and losing hurts. Insist upon 'thank you for playing' and 'congratulations' at the conclusion of play.

4. Positive about Yourself

Keep the children in a circle and begin by saying something positive about yourself. Maintain eye contact with the group whilst you are doing it. For instance, 'I like myself because I try to be happy all the time.' Then ask a child on your left or right to say something positive about themselves. At first the children will probably say something about liking their trainers. Let this go at first but slowly and gently push for something about them as people. Saying something like: 'Yes, I like your trainers too, but try to think of something you like about your personality, not about something that you are wearing.' If you have a child that is reluctant the following approach is sometimes useful, say something like, 'Tyreka is having trouble with this one, lets help her out and all say something positive about her.'

This will immerse Tyreka in a sea of positive language about herself and give her some ideas. If this still fails, pick two of the positives that she has heard from the group and offer a choice. Something like, 'OK Tyreka you have nice hair and a great smile which one do you want to say?' If that doesn't work leave the child for that week. They will think about it before the next group and say something next time the group meets.

Anger Management Cards

Walk away.	Try to relax.
Say some positive things to yourself.	Take deep controlled breaths.
Sing a song in your head.	Count backwards from twenty.
Use a magic word in your head (for example, stop or calm).	Imagine a soothing scene in your head (for example, floating in the sea).

Chapter 7

Session 10: Mini Group Sessions

Materials and Resources

Flipchart.

Pen.

The end of term is a good time to begin to wind down the group. However, do not leave the children up in the air. They will have treasured this group and the support it has given them. It is essential that they feel it is still there for them. You can run this session as quite a fun session in ten minutes or so and repeat it as often as necessary. I call these mini group sessions contact groups because you are letting the children know that you are still interested and you do this by keeping in contact.

Sample Contact Group Session

1. Check In

This is a simple but essential component of any group that seeks to be supportive. Each member of the group takes their turn to report on their week. Instigate this by asking an age appropriate question such as, 'Has anybody got any news?' or 'How have things been?' With an anger management group this will become the core component of the group's work. This is the time when the children will tell you about the difficult situations they have been in during the week. If they don't you will no doubt be aware from your own observations or from other staff that there have been some difficulties. You can bring these up if the child doesn't. The way I tackle the problems that are discussed is to give the group a summary of the child's account of the event and ask if anyone can suggest how this situation could have been handled. The whole group is then immersed in a sea of words that will encourage the development of a more complex array of strategies for coping with situations. You may need to note down the alternative options and then one by one ask the group to predict the outcome of each alternative, in its fullest sense. For instance, 'What would be likely to happen if John told the teacher that Tom had spat at him?' 'Tom would get in trouble,' 'John would be allowed to go to the toilet and clean himself up.'

2. I Made a Good Choice

This game reinforces 'The Interview' and gives the children the opportunity to receive acclaim for being in a difficult situation and making a good choice. Try to get the children to detail the range of choices they had available to them. A typical interaction between the child, facilitator and group might go like this:

Child: The time I made a choice was last week when John came up to me in class and whispered, 'Your mum raids bins for your dinner.' I just sat there.

Facilitator: How did you feel?

Child: I felt angry and wanted to get up and hit him.

Facilitator:	What choices did you have?
Child:	Tell the teacher or ignore him.
Facilitator (to group):	Did (target child) have any other choices?
Member of group:	He could have hit him or shouted at him.
Facilitator (to group):	Seems like (target child) made a great choice. Let's all shake his hand and say well done.

You can extend this activity by getting the children in the group or the target child to predict what the consequences would have been had they chosen any of the other options. This may seem a little long-winded, but as the pupils get into the swing of this they become very adept at it, which is what you are aiming at. The children should be able to think very quickly about what will happen if they make a choice and thus begin to make the choices that are in their best interests, and keep them out of trouble.

3. Remember When

The children absolutely love this game. It is rather like a parent telling their own children about the funny things that the children did when they were little. Begin by saying something like, 'Michael do you remember when I observed you in class and you were hiding under the table?' This is said with much mirth and fondness. This is not to say that one is condoning the behaviour. What you are saying is that the behaviour is so far in the past that a repetition is unthinkable now and so it is OK to laugh about it. This in itself reinforces the extinguishing of the behaviour, because they would really let you down if it ever reappeared.

4. A Positive Game

That is:

- positive about yourself (Session One)
- positive about someone I dislike (Session Five)
- positive about school (Session Seven).

5. Firm Handshake and Farewell

Here you are seeking to develop a firm assertive handshake with eye contact. Remember many of the children in an anger management group will not have developed assertive skills. They may know how to be submissive when confronted with a much stronger adversary or how to give an aggressive hard stare. So don't be surprised if this comes a little difficult at first. Model this by holding out your hand whilst making eye contact and saying, 'Thank you for all your hard work today.' Expect the children to make eye contact with you and to maintain eye contact during the interaction and say quietly yet firmly, 'Thank you.' After a while the children get really good at this and you can do a round of hand shaking very quickly

6. Closure

You will need to acknowledge that the group is ending. You will need to discuss how you feel about it and model the right kind of behaviour by sending 'I' messages about your own feelings on leaving the group. You will need to acknowledge too that some pupils may express anger whereas others may be relieved that they will be able to escape from the emotional involvement that a good group member requires, and some will have a mixture of these two emotions. You should be willing to accept all of these feelings.

Some pupils may want to thank the group for accepting and helping them. Others may wish to apologise to the individuals they have offended in the past or may wish to explain certain aspects of their behaviour that they did not feel free to discuss in previous sessions. It is best to end the group with as little as possible unfinished business!

However, it is important to discuss with the group what personal resources they might call upon should a new or recurring problem arise, obviously the Anger Management Cards are a starting point, together with relaxation and visualisation. You might also want to discuss what other resources they might want to use, such as friends and school staff.

It is always a positive move to celebrate any achievements. Certificates should comment on weekly improvements and can therefore be used in the format provided (page 131) or a revised version can be presented at the end of the intervention programme. All of the certificates should be presented by senior staff at an appropriate assembly.

Certificate of Improvement

This is to say that

....

has improved in school this week.

Particularly in:

....

....

Date ....

Signed ....

Post-Intervention Measures

These would be identical to the pre-intervention measures and would compare any changes in the ratings pre- and post the intervention of the anger management programme. So, for example, if the Behaviour Checklist for staff to complete about children and young people was used, any drop in the percentages of the individual measures (interactions with staff, attitudes to other pupils and personal ways) for each of the pupils on the programme would represent an improvement in behaviour from the staff perspective. The scores also highlight specific behaviours which help in making sense of pre-and post-interventions.

The average percentages for all three measures could also be used. For the 'My Hot Spots' questionnaire for pupils, we would be looking for a drop in individual ratings for each of the listed statements about what things made the pupil angry and what the pupil's did to make other people angry.

With the SDQ it is probably best to look for drops in the total scores for teacher and pupil ratings pre and post the intervention programme. If you have a member of staff with a knowledge of statistics then the pre- and post numbers could be compared for any significant statistical difference.

Summary

This chapter has provided an eight session anger management group intervention programme with support and two mini-group sessions to facilitate group closure. Post-programme measures are particularly important for demonstrating the success or otherwise of such interventions.

Questions for You to Consider

- When will you take the post intervention measures – after Session Eight or after the support and mini-group sessions?

- How will you feedback your evaluation of the pre- and post-intervention measures to the pupils, other staff and parents/carers?

- When and how will you give the pupils their certificates?

- How will you ensure that progress made is maintained?

Chapter 8: Intervening with Individual Children and Young People

Much of the theoretical framework for understanding and responding to anger management in this book has its roots in Cognitive Behaviour Therapy.

When CBT is used with children and young people it is important to:

- Be specific by selecting one behaviour to work on first.

- Be positive by noticing and rewarding all acceptable behaviours – that is, 'catching them being good'.

- Be consistent because everyone needs to know that 'if this happens, then this is going to happen next'.

- Be patient because behaviour changes slowly at first and everyone needs support when starting a behaviour management programme.

The application of CBT theory to anger management approaches with individual children is described in this chapter in terms of behaviour contracts and Positive Psychology. The use of both contacts and Positive Psychology helps us to move away from problem-focused or child-deficit models of behaviour towards desirable positive behaviours that promote the development of psychological wellbeing and resilience in children and young people. Wellbeing can be defined as a positive and sustainable condition that allows individuals to thrive and flourish. It also encompasses resilience, which is the ability to cope well in the face of adversity, such as when feeling threatened, and enables an individual to maintain a positive sense of self (Huppert, Baylis & Keverne, 2005). This focus draws on the key underlying principles of the Positive Psychology movements (Linley & Joseph, 2004; Seligman & Csikszentmihalyi, 2000) and resilience research (Bernard, 2004; Haggerty, et al. 1996). These approaches recognise the existence of adversities and developmental challenges that affect many children in different ways but also share an optimistic perspective for optimising true wellbeing for both individuals and their (school) communities. Such an orientation towards resilience and wellbeing asserts that all children have the potential for 'good' and are motivated to pursue a 'good life' and that the undertakings and (formal or informal) contractual agreements between the child and the many systems in their lives (such as their family, peers, school) play a role in that child's development. This is in contrast to the medical (or 'disease') model that focuses on identifying and treating difficulties within the individual where there is often a framework of despair and a culture of complaint. Blaming parents and professional feelings of disempowerment by their organisations are two key features.

Within the medical model, negatively stereotyping children with anger management problems creates reinforcement amongst their peers which can in turn encourage further social negativity towards the stigmatised (angry) child. To counter such negativity we must encourage staff working with children to identify and develop the positive attributes that all children possess.

8

Contracts

One approach to helping pupils manage their anger better in the classroom is through the use of 'contingency contracting'. The use of a contract is based on the assumption that an individual's interaction (or exchange) with his environment is based on actions that will bring about the greatest relative advantage or the least relative disadvantage in the fulfillment of his needs. A contract, even a simple one: 'If you do this, I'll do that,' verbally or written provides a statement of the rights and obligations of all parties to the contract. The value of behaviour (its price) is measured in terms of what the individual has to give up for it. So, for example, if you ask a child to give up behaving in a certain way, he must get something of value to him for that exchange. We all exchange behaviours in this way and most of us are fortunate enough to have a written contract stating the terms of our employment: what duties we are to perform, for what period and for what compensation (pay).

The advantages of contingency contracting follow:

- The child plays an active role.

- The teacher collects information about the child's progress in managing their anger based on, say, the frequency of their past outbursts of temper and their present outbursts or lack of them.

- The teacher encourages the child to choose realistic targets and desirable rewards and makes sure that the relationship between achieving targets and rewards is realistic: this means that the number of targets to be achieved before earning the reward must be within the child's capabilities as failure right at the beginning is likely to de-motivate. Making it too easy to earn rewards can de-value both the rewards and the whole process of contingency contracting.

Contracts contain five elements:

1. Contracts should detail the rewards each person expects to gain from the contract, for example, teachers or parents may want a child to play appropriately with other children or stay in the classroom rather than run out when angry. On the other hand, the child wants free time with friends, games, toys, other equipment and so on. So if, for example, after every ten minutes that the teacher looks at Tracy and she is on-task (working) rather than arguing with other children, the teacher will say: 'Well done Tracy for working, you've earned a star and some free time to play with...' If Darren raises his hand to ask a question and waits until he is asked to speak rather than not engage with the discussion because he is angry about something that went on outside of class, he obtains a positive comment on his report card and 'n' number of positive comments can be 'cashed in' for a special treat at home.

2. The target behaviour for a child must be SMART (specific, measurable, achievable, resourced and time-limited). So, for example, if parents or teachers cannot determine whether an obligation has been met or if a child cannot manage their angry outbursts more frequently and/or appropriately, then a privilege cannot be granted. You should decide what you want to see the child doing, in a set period of time, and this should be expressed in a positive way. For example, 'for Tracy to work alongside Darren for ten minutes without engaging in physical contact' as opposed to 'Tracy will stop interrupting Darren when they are working together'. You will also need to decide whether or not any resources are required.

In the example just given, the resources are that you will need to check every ten minutes that Tracy is working appropriately alongside Darren.

3. The consequences for sticking or not sticking to the terms of the contract must be clearly spelt out with rewards and sanctions planned and agreed by all parties in advance as well as being applied consistently and systematically. There should not be any arbitrary or 'post facto' arrangements. You must agree on what staff are going to do if the identified inappropriate behaviour occurs. So if, for example, Tracy hits Darren she is immediately asked to move to another desk by herself away from Darren for five minutes. If Darren interrupts the lesson because he is angry about something, ignore him and continue with the lesson.

Before you initiate the contract you will need to make sure that the pupil is aware of the general classroom rules and the specific expectations you have of his behaviour, especially when he is upset or annoyed about something or someone. Explain to him that what he is doing is not acceptable and what the consequences will be. Remember that we are trying to increase acceptable behaviours and that the pupil must at all times be able to earn rewards either in the form of social praise or social praise paired with a tangible reward. If you are going to use a tangible reward then you must explain to the pupil how such a reward can be earned.

4. A contract can provide a bonus clause so that extra activities, extensions of free time and so on are available as rewards for consistence performance over a prolonged period. Consistent performance (for example, controlling one's anger) often goes un-reinforced in everyday life because it gets overlooked and because teachers often expect such performances to occur ordinarily with questions such as: 'Why should I reward him for what he should be doing anyway?' For a child whose desirable behaviour has been recently acquired, it is crucial for teachers to provide reinforcement for consistent performance and bonuses written in the contract can serve such a purpose.

5. Contracts should be made for short periods of say a week or two in order to allow for revision, that is, to maybe change the target criteria or reward schedules. In this way, a contract should provide a means of monitoring the rate of positive reinforcement given and received. The records that are kept inform each party of the progress (or lack of it) within the contractual programme.

8

Contract

I, Darren, during the next two weeks will try to manage my frustration better when I am not given immediate teacher attention or when I am reprimanded for shouting out answers during class discussions.
I will do this by doing the following:

- Putting my hand up if I have a question to ask or if I want to answer a question.

- Waiting until Mr Greaves says my name and asks me what my question is or asks me to answer his question.

- If I do not have a question to ask or have an answer to one of Mr Greaves' questions I will sit quietly and listen to the class discussion.

During the next two weeks Mr Greaves will try to help me to manage my frustration better during class discussions.

He will do this by doing the following:

- Telling me by name that he has seen me with my hand up and either asking me to say what I wanted to say or telling me when I will be able to have my say.

- Praising me by name, for example, 'Well done Darren for putting up your hand to ask/answer a question.'

- Praising me for sitting quietly during class discussions when I don't have a question to ask or answer.

- By giving me a star every time I put up my hand to ask or answer a question.

- By giving me a star for every time I sit quietly during class discussions when I don't have a question to ask or answer.

Every five stars that I earn can be exchanged for ten minutes on the computer to play a game of my choice either at lunch times or during Friday afternoon's class choice time. My bonus for keeping strictly to the contract for the entire period will be that Mr Greaves will send an 'improved behaviour' certificate home to my mum at the end of the week. My mum will let me stay up for an extra hour on Saturday night.
If I do not put up my hand to ask or answer a question or if I do not sit quietly and listen during class discussions I will be given three verbal reminders by Mr Greaves saying that I am not behaving as agreed in this contract. After the third warning I will be asked to go to the headteacher's room for the remainder of the lesson. This will mean that I will not be able to earn any stars and exchange them for time on the computer and I will not be able to earn any bonus for the week.

Signed: ....
Darren (pupil)

Signed: ....
Mr Greaves (teacher)

Signed: ....
Ms Bent (parent)

Date: ....

Evaluating the Contract

If after a week or two there has been an increase in the desirable (target) behaviour (or a decrease in unwanted behaviour) then all parties can say 'well done' to each other. You will now have to decide whether to introduce a second problem behaviour to tackle. In Darren's case the second behaviour might be starting a written task after the first time of being asked by the teacher, this behaviour could incorporate the hand raising element of the first contract if Darren has a question to ask. The teacher's helpful behaviour here would be to acknowledge and praise Darren for putting up his hand. Darren could earn and exchange stars in a similar fashion to the first contract.

However, if the contractual programme has not been effective then you will need to check the following:

- Are the rewards rewarding? Maybe, for example, there needs to be a previously agreed 'menu of rewards' from which Darren could pick – this would add some variety.

- Is the programme being carried out consistently and systematically? In Darren's case is the teacher noticing and praising Darren for having his hand up? Sometimes when teachers ignore children with their hands up the children put them down again and either refuse to participate any more or else simply mess about.

- Are the sanctions (for not sticking to the contract) effective? Perhaps, in Darren's case, it is rewarding for him to spend some one-to-one time with the headteacher, especially if the headteacher is giving Darren lots of attention.

If none of the above appear to be contributing to contract programme failure then you should re-examine the priority problem (maybe it is not as amenable to change as first thought). Maybe Darren should be sitting closer to the teacher during whole-class discussions. Maybe Darren could be reminded to raise his hand before asking or answering a question and then praised and rewarded (with a star) the next time he engages in this behaviour without prompting.

Practising Writing Contracts

A facilitator working with a group of staff using the activity page, 'Writing Contracts: Identifying the Behaviours' (page 149), could ask the whole staff group to generate a list of inappropriate classroom behaviours associated with loss of control that pupils have or have attempted to display in their classes when they have become angry or have been frustrated about something.

The staff group, working in pairs, would then be given one of these behaviours by the facilitator to re-write in positive terms as a target behaviour related to managing anger. So, for example, the behaviour 'makes others angry when working in small groups' could be re-drafted as 'engages positively and co-operatively with others during small group work'. Each pair would then be asked to describe specific behaviours needed to reach the target behaviour that would illustrate their re-drafted desired positive behaviour. So the behaviours that might illustrate co-operative small group behaviour could include:

8

- Listening while others in the group are talking.

- Waiting to take his turn before talking.

- Helping others who are having difficulty with the task.

- Allowing someone else in the group to feedback the group's work to the class.

Using the activity page 'Writing Contracts: Reinforcing the Behaviours' (page 150) each pair of staff would then be asked to describe some teacher behaviours to reinforce the target behaviour So, in the example above it might be:

- Spend some time observing the group and awarding stars for the target child when he was listening, turn-taking, helping and so on.

- Observe the target child's behaviour from a distance.

- Praise the target child for these desired behaviours.

Finally, each pair would be asked to provide a written list for a possible menu of rewards that could be used, together with suggestions for a bonus for the pupil meeting all the desired behaviours during say a week as well as listing the possible consequences that could be applied for the pupil not sticking to the agreement.

The facilitator would take feedback from the pairs depending on the amount of time available.

Positive Psychology and Cognitive Behaviour Therapy

Positive Psychology is primarily concerned with happiness and strengths as well as children's resilience to negative life events including those that may lead a young person choosing to respond in an aggressive or angry manner. Positive Psychology is about what makes life worth living (Peterson & Park, 2003). It has emerged as a reaction to the child-deficit or 'medical' model described in the introduction to this chapter. A number of interpersonal qualities have been identified as playing a central role in Positive Psychology which include: strengths of character and virtues such as creativity and curiosity (Seligman, 2003) and positive emotions, such as enjoying making things better, wanting to work with others (Snyder & Lopez, 2002). Personality traits such as agreeability and conscientiousness can often have a positive impact on social situations, such as group or classroom activities (Park, Peterson & Seligman, 2004).

Because Positive Psychology seeks to adopt preventative measures by building from a baseline of mentally healthy children and young people, a focus on positive interpersonal qualities provides valuable anger management interventions if the interpersonal qualities are systematically identified in each pupil and built upon. It is the extent and manner in which interpersonal qualities are exhibited that may contribute towards successful anger management interventions. For example, some pupils may think of themselves as an accepting person and yet still lose their temper if they perceive things as not going their way. In such situations they are not accepting and are not thinking about why they are not accepting. Instead we could encourage pupils to think about how they could use their interpersonal qualities in a new way (to control their temper) by engaging them in activities that are meaningful to them.

Karwoski et al. (2006) have identified particular elements of CBT that are consistent with Positive Psychology, that is:

1. A focus on assisting in the achievement of a happier life and not just focusing on 'fixing problems'.

2. A focus on discrete and meaningful goals rather than broad-based 'therapy'.

3. Realistic and positive reframing of negative thoughts to reduce negative emotions.

4. A focus on developing competency in helpful and reality-based thinking as a buffer to future problems.

5. Scheduling of pleasant activities accompanied by mood monitoring.

Karwoski et al. (2006) have argued for the integration of more Positive Psychology elements within the CBT approach. In particular they advocate an emphasis on identifying and cultivating individual latent strengths, especially those that may have been compromised by stress and adversity, and the enhancement of positive emotions via optimistic thinking and the development of a strong sense of meaning and purpose.

Some simple exercises and ideas follow to demonstrate how Positive Psychology can be applied to working with individual young people to help them to manage their behaviour more appropriately. It is suggested that the facilitator encourage staff to try out each of these exercises and then to discuss, at a future meeting or meetings of the staff group, their possible adaptation and/or modification for use with pupils where this is not already suggested in the text.

1. Focusing on Achieving a Happier Life Rather than 'Fixing Problems'

A happy life is one in which good feelings or pleasure is maximised and bad feelings or pain are minimised. In this sense happiness is the sum over a lifetime of all these specific feelings and what Kahneman (1999) has described as a 'bottom-up' approach to explaining happiness. By contrast, a second theory of happiness is 'desire theory', which holds that happiness is a matter of getting what you want, whether or not it involves pleasure (Griffin, 1986).

A third theory (Nussbaum, 1992) has emerged because what we want may strike others as shallow or inconsequential. This theory is known as the 'objective list theory' and suggests that what is intrinsically good for us, good for its own sake rather than as a means to an end, is to get or achieve what has intrinsic value irrespective of who or what we are. There really are some truly valuable things in the world that would be included on this list, such as: health, material comfort, a good career, friendship, children, education and so on, and happiness entails achieving a number of these things. According to Peterson (2006) the best theory may be one that somehow combines these different explanations of happiness and that measurements of happiness can only be a subjective experience.

Any one or more of these activities can be tried as a means of 'boosting' happiness:

a) Have a good day.

In a notebook keep a track of what you do during a day. Some people find it easy to keep a diary on an hour-to-hour basis, whereas others prefer to summarise their day in terms of its dominant features: this would certainly be true of young people and for some they may need some help and encouragement to remember what happened during any

8

given day! Regardless, at the end of the day, write down an overall rating using the rating scale.

1 = It was one of the worst days of my life.

2 = It was a terrible day.

3 = It was a bad day.

4 = It was a below average day.

5 = It was an average or typical day.

6 = It was a good day.

7 = It was a very good day.

8 = It was an excellent day.

9 = It was an outstanding day.

10 = It was one of the best days of my life.

Do this for two to four weeks and do not review your record until the end of the period. Go back over the record and look for a pattern across the days and weeks. Compare good days with bad days in terms of what you were doing or not doing on those days – a pattern should emerge.

b) Three good things.

At the end of each day write down three things that went well during the day. Do this every day for a week. The three things you list can be relatively small (for example, for pupils it might be something like 'my mum bought me sweets on the way home from school') or relatively large in importance (for example, for pupils it might be something like 'my sister graduated from college'). After each positive point on your list, answer in your own words the question: 'Why did this good thing happen?' For the examples just given the pupils might say, 'Because I had a good day at school,' and 'Because she worked really hard and revised for her exams.'

c) You at your best.

Write a story about an event that brought the best out in you. Answer in your own words the question: 'Why did this good thing happen?' Then keep a diary of every good thing that happens to you during the next week.

2. Focusing on Meaningful Goals Rather than Broad-Based Remedies

In Positive Psychology such a focus is often associated with wellnesses and wellness promotion. According to Peterson (2006) wellness results from a healthy lifestyle with sustained habits (having a balanced diet) as opposed to singular events (seeking weight loss). Peterson suggests that discussions of mental health have lagged behind discussions of physical health for all the reasons that Positive Psychology and its focus on doing well have been neglected. Peterson also alludes to the fact that even children often regarded as psychologically vulnerable, even fragile, can often overcome adversity and thrive, and quotes longitudinal research in the 1980's (Garmezy, 1983) in which some, though not all, showed resistance to life's most severe stressors, flourishing in spite of every prediction to the contrary.

Werner (1982) obtained the same results and adopted the term 'resiliency' to describe the quality that enables many young people to thrive in the face of adversity. It would seem from the more recent work of Bernard (1991) that resiliency amongst children and young people incorporates perseverance, having a sense of purpose through clear and coherent target setting and a self-belief in achieving these targets, especially those relating to education.

To demonstrate this approach you may want to think about a habitual behaviour that you want to reduce or eliminate, or a new behaviour that you want to add to your repertoire. The habit may be, for example, arriving at meetings late and being unprepared, when you may actually want to give yourself enough time to both prepare for the meeting as well as arrive on time. There is an overlap here with contingency contracting described earlier.

Sometimes you can do both at the same time, and you may actually want to do so, under the assumption that the bad habit may serve some purpose for you. For example, arriving late at meetings and being unprepared may give you an excuse not to participate because of your lack of knowledge about the subject matter on the agenda. You can, of course, use preparing for the meeting as an excuse for arriving late when in fact there were other reasons for your lateness. Merely eliminating the bad habit of arriving late to meetings and being unprepared can leave that purpose hanging (that is, the need for better personal planning and time management) and may result in you drifting back into the bad habit of lateness and a lack of preparation.

For children and young people they may say that they want to stop losing their temper and yet they don't say what behaviour they want to add to their repertoire.

It is important to define the habit for yourself in concrete ways that allow you to monitor changes (and the same would be true of the pupil who has temper tantrums). 'Becoming a better teacher' is a wonderful goal, but it is a lot easier to know you have succeeded at 'greeting your class every morning'. Along these lines, it is easier to change a habit that allows you to do so in small steps, so that you can note and congratulate yourself on your progress.

The same is true of children and young people, for example, becoming a calmer pupil may be an excellent goal, only it is much easier for the pupil to know that he has succeeded at not getting upset every time things don't go his way. This is why contingency contracts with certificates or letters home can be such a powerful reinforcer. It is much easier for a pupil to change his temper tantrum habit by allowing himself to do so in small steps, so that he notes and congratulates himself every time he responds calmly when the outcome of a situation is not as he might have wanted.

You will probably want to get into the practice of keeping a diary with regard to whatever habit you want to change.

Young people can be helped to self-monitor their behaviour in a similar way. If you want children to reduce their temper tantrums, they can record how many times they lost their temper at the end of the day. It is a good idea to keep a diary for a week or two before you try to change the habit. This will give you a good idea of what the habit entails. Expect some backsliding (that is, a return to temper tantrums) because making change is never as difficult as maintaining the change, whenever the steps taken to change a habit prove impossible to incorporate into your lifestyle. So while you think of how to change the habit, also keep in mind what you will do to keep the change permanent. We need to ask young people what they think they need to do to keep any change permanent and we should not urge them to do their best but rather to succeed.

8

3. Reframing Negative Thoughts and Emotions

There is ample reason to believe that optimism is useful because positive expectations can be self-fulfilling. Gillham et al. (1995) created an intervention called the Penn Resiliency Programme (PRP) and used strategies from cognitive behaviour therapy to teach primary aged children to be more optimistic as measured by the PRP. Peterson (2006) suggests that optimism can be acquired through modelling and if so we need to be attentive to the messages young people get about the world and how it works.

Although there are plenty of reasons to be optimistic, urging you to be more hopeful is as empty as saying 'don't worry, be happy'. What you need in reality is strategies for putting such advice into action. Strategies involved in the PRP take place over an extended period of time and usually involve a trusted facilitator who leads individuals through the necessary steps, devising and evaluating assignments in which various strategies for thinking more optimistically are perfected.

Learning to be optimistic is hard work and takes much practice to perfect. The following activities present a facilitator of a staff group with one such technique to try out and to discuss its appropriateness for use with pupils. The technique is based on the premise that what spirals people into a bad mood or worse following a setback is a pessimistic style of thinking about that setback. This thinking style is then carried into the future where it demoralises that person in other situations. The person needs to interrupt his immediate reaction to a setback and then think about it in a less-pessimistic way.

The facilitator would say to a staff group:

'Suppose a member of staff senior to you passes you in the corridor without saying hello or even acknowledging you. That, of course, makes you feel bad, but then what?'

The staff group would be asked to brainstorm in three's or four's what a pessimistic person might say to himself in such a situation and the facilitator would then take feedback from each group.

Possible responses from the staff group might be:

- She hates me.
- I deserve to be hated.
- I am a complete loser and she knows it.
- If only I was more intelligent this would not happen to me.
- I will never be a good teacher.

Assuming that these comments are not a realistic appraisal, the facilitator would then say:

'Let's assume that you are intelligent and you are a good teacher. What you need to do in this case is to head off your negative speculative spiral before it goes too far. Are there different and more optimistic ways to make sense of being ignored?'

The staff group would be asked to brainstorm in threes or fours what an optimistic person might say to himself in such a situation and the facilitator would then take feedback from each group.

Possible responses from the staff group might be:

- She was having a bad day.
- She was in a hurry.
- She was thinking about something else.
- She wasn't wearing her glasses so maybe she didn't see me.

One of the PRP techniques designed to offer optimistic interpretations in the moment (Reivich, Gillham & Shatte, 2004) is called the 'hot seat technique' or sometimes the 'rapid fire technique'. The intention is to teach people how to quickly challenge pessimistic thoughts. It is a powerful strategy for learning optimism that develops through trying it out, especially as people do not naturally challenge their thinking.

Practising the hot seat technique:

The facilitator would ask the staff group to individually list common events that make them feel angry or upset, such as not being given an opportunity to voice an opinion in staff meetings. These would all be listed on a flipchart to check for duplicity and clarity. An agreed shortlist of 12 events would then be drawn up. The staff group would be asked to work in pairs and would have 12 index cards: they would write one of these 12 events on each card. One member of the pair would choose one of the index cards and read it aloud to his partner

The partner would then try to identify the immediate automatic and pessimistic thoughts that the event triggers and then as rapidly as possible do one of these three things (the examples are based on being ignored in the corridor):

1. Evaluate the evidence for the pessimistic thought: 'Am I going to get reprimanded by my Head of Department? Probably not because I had a good performance management meeting last week.'

2. Think of an alternative explanation: 'The member of staff (senior to me) is not one for making small talk.'

3. Put the thought in perspective: 'The staff I work with at school are not my family and besides my wife and kids love me.'

A second, third and fourth card would be chosen and of course the pair can swap over. This activity could be repeated at other staff training times.

The staff group can be asked how they might want to re-word the above phrases, relating to the senior member of staff ignoring them, for pupils and may want to think about how they would model examples for them. For example, a pupil's pessimistic thought might be, 'Am I going to get in trouble for arguing with my teacher about not completing my classwork? Probably not because I got a good mark in the test last week.' As an alternative to arguing with the teacher, the pupil could offer to finish off his work at lunchtime. And putting the thought into perspective the pupil might say to himself: 'At least I know how to complete the work and I can do it in my own time.'

8

There are, of course, some caveats for both staff and pupils. There is the possibility that your pessimistic reaction contains a gram of truth. A related pitfall in developing and using the 'hot seat technique' is that a bad situation is minimised to the point of denying its significance. Although many of the optimistic examples offered above appropriately turn events back on other people or circumstances, being optimistic is not the same as shirking your responsibilities.

4. Focusing on Developing Competencies for Problem-Solving

Almost 50 years ago, Robert White (1959) introduced the concept of competence, arguing that people are motivated to behave in a competent way, regardless of what they are doing. However, competence is a different sort of motive because it is never described in the same way as say hunger or thirst. We experience pleasure in doing things well regardless of what else our behaviour produces (Meier, 1993).

Remember the first time you learned how to drive or send an e-mail or text message? These probably simply felt good. Competence may be fulfilling because it provides insight into the sorts of activities in which we are attracted: they must afford opportunities for acquiring skilled performance and thus allow improvement. Something we can do perfectly well the first time we try is unlikely to become a lifelong interest.

Howard Gardener's (1983) theory of multiple intelligences suggests that intelligence is a set of problem-solving skills that allows us to resolve the difficulties we encounter. Gardener speculated that seven basic abilities arose in the course of evolution and that these skills are independent of each other. Gardener's (1991) alternative to formal assessment is 'assessment in context' in that information about a person's abilities can be obtained in the course of their everyday activities.

Gardener's (1983) seven multiple intelligences are:

1. Linguistic: sensitivity to the meanings and functions of language as illustrated by poets and lyricists.

2. Logical-mathematical: competence in organising ideas in abstract ways as demonstrated by mathematicians and theoretical physicists.

3. Spatial: capacity for visual or spatial imagery, including the ability to transform images usually shown by navigators, football players and sculptors.

4. Musical: ability to produce and organise sounds according to prescribed pitch and rhythm as displayed by musicians.

5. Bodily: kinesthetic mastery over body movements, usually present in dancers, surgeons and athletes.

6. Personal: ability to assess own feelings often associated by introspective novelists.

7. Social: ability to understand other people and what motivates them often displayed by politicians, religious leaders, and salespeople.

Capitalising on your Interests and Abilities

The activities that follow are for staff who could then think about how to guide their pupils through similar activities. The exercises would be led through a facilitator who would ask staff to participate individually and share their response with one or two other colleagues. Whole-group feedback would be taken to discuss the value of the exercises for use with pupils. As a cautionary note, these exercises will fail if staff are too literal or concrete in identifying their interests and abilities. For example, simply recounting or providing a verbatim account of what they did during a particular evening or over a weekend or a longer break from school.

As an activity for you as the reader, you could identify your interests by keeping a daily or weekly diary of how you spend your leisure time and then try to identify any themes that underlie your leisure activities that might be helpful in meeting future problems associated with your teaching and work in school. For example, going cycling over the weekend gives you time alone that helps you relax and allows you to let your mind wander. In relation to work in school it is akin to removing yourself from situations to have time alone to think and plan ahead one thing at a time.

As a further activity for you as the reader to identify your abilities you must first be honest with yourself about what you do well in terms of Gardener's (1983) seven multiple intelligences and remember that Gardener emphasises actual accomplishments so you need to pay attention to what you have achieved in your life so far. For example, are you an accomplished musician or poet (linguistic and musical intelligences)? Do you excel at sports (spatial or bodily intelligences)? Are you competent at organising your ideas and thoughts (logical-mathematical intelligence)? Have others commented on your ability to understand, to be in touch with your own feelings and to know what motivates them (personal and social intelligences)? If an answer is not immediate, use Gardener's idea that people with a given intelligence, balance its use in relation to the other intelligences. So, think of films you have seen or books you have read in which a given character has struck you as memorable or admirable. Look beyond their physical appearance and life style to see if there is a common intelligence. In other words, what has attracted you about the lead characters, authors, directors and so on, for example: their sensitivity to the meanings and functions (linguistic intelligence) or their ability to understand other people and what motivates them (social intelligence).

Once you have identified an interest or ability you could ask yourself how you can use it at work in a different way, in your teaching or in your interactions with others. You might want to think about how you use posters and visual displays in class: will they be solely in linguistic terms or will they show your spatial intelligence in the way in which you transform the images. Will you include practical demonstrations in your teaching (bodily intelligence)? Will you use music or have stories on tape to help improve children's listening skills (musical intelligence)? Will you volunteer to support a colleague who is having some problems with a difficult class (social intelligence)?

Follow this idea through for at least a week and ask yourself whether or not you are happier than you were before starting these exercises (personal intelligence). Understanding your own intelligences can help you to understand the intelligences of children and young people, especially if you want to intervene with an angry child. For example, for an angry child with a high degree of musical intelligence you may want to play him some music of which you are familiar, especially if it is music that is both current and that has helped you to relax and ask him the following questions:

- What colours do you imagine as you are listening to the music?

- If you could touch the music, what would it feel like?

- How do you feel as you listen to the music?

- What is this music about?

- What do you think the people in the music are feeling?

Questions such as these use the angry child's musical intelligence to get in touch with his other senses and feelings which could be used to help him to relax in confrontational situations with others.

5. Finding Time for Pleasant Activities

Finding time for pleasant activities is an important individual intervention for young people as it shifts the focus away from the unpleasant consequences resulting from angry outbursts or temper tantrums. It is also acknowledged that some of the consequences may result in a positive outcome for the young person, especially if they get what they want.

Pleasure too is multidimensional because even though we may offer summary judgements of pleasure, we can simultaneously experience positive and negative feelings. 'Bittersweet' describes a taste that is both bad and good and is an apt metaphor for many of our experiences. Although we often focus on pleasure in the here and now we may also experience pleasurable memories of the past and we may have particular hopes for the future.

Psychologists have distinguished a whole family of positive feelings that include pleasurable sensations, emotions, moods and so on, and these too can be contrasted with unpleasant experiences of a temper tantrum. There is general agreement amongst psychologists that feelings differ with respect to how long they last, their attachment to particular events and situations and their complexity, that is, the degree to which psychological processes are involved in their experience (Larsen & Frederickson, 1999).

Pleasures like temper outbursts are often brief, tied to specific events and simple, whereas emotions such as anger are more complex in that they don't just involve subjective feelings but also characteristic patterns of physiological arousal, thoughts and behaviours and 'anger' displays all of these characteristics, as has been previously described in the firework model.

The term mood sometimes refers to a constricted emotion: 'I was in the mood for a fight', but an additional and more substantive meaning emphasises the role of mood in general wellbeing. We speak of people as being good-natured or irritable; mellow or bad-tempered and so on, and we apply these terms to their entire personality. With anger this often results in negative stereotyping and fits into a child-deficit medical model described in the introduction to this chapter.

To apply psychological jargon, moods (as in being in the mood for a fight) can be defined as 'trait-like' whereas emotions (feeling angry) are 'state-like'. Moods are less likely to have a specific object or meaning associated with them and they are less likely to be at the centre of our consciousness. However, moods are longer lasting than emotions and they colour all of what we think and feel.

'Savouring' refers to our awareness of pleasure and our deliberate attempt to make it last. Some children will of course get a deliberate pleasure out of being angry and losing their temper especially if it gets them what they want or conforms to what they think others expect of them. Angry children may also set out to engage in provocative acts designed to make themselves outcasts as a means of relief from their anxiety over relationships with adults based on previous rejections. The use of behavioural contracts is the means by which adults can help young people to regain their trust in them because the contract sets out an agreement for all parties and sets out the terms for the agreement.

Bryant (2003) contrasts savouring with 'coping' and says that in coping we experience a bad event that produces negative feelings such as anxiety and sadness, and we attempt to 'deal with' these feelings in a variety of ways. We may try to change the event itself or its consequences or we may try to change ourselves. Sometimes we cope with life's triumphs and pleasures by referring to a maxim learned years ago that reminds us that pride goes before a fall enabling us to remain happy. We may worry that others will resent us or we may conclude that we are lucky or that we have set a standard impossible to maintain.

Coping is very much linked with resilience in that the better we cope the more resilient we become. Nevertheless, Bryant (2003) has determined that our habitual predisposition to relish or not is relatively stable and that savouring is a good thing, provided that what is savored is socially appropriate.

A facilitator could use the following activity with a staff group for them to use with their pupils. He would say to the staff group: 'Think about a time when something was good or pleasurable. It could be a great meal, an engaging conversation or a spontaneous adventure.' For young people a good time or pleasurable experience may relate to getting a certificate or being praised for good work. This would perhaps be in contrast with the unpleasant experiences surrounding temper tantrums.

The following strategies, which do not have to be followed in sequence, would then be followed by individuals in the group:

1. Sharing with others: working in pairs or threes each person would share the experience or simply tell others how much you valued the moment.

2. Developing your memory: take mental photographs or even think of a physical souvenir of the event and reminisce about it. (This could be done alone as a self-reflection and maybe sharing with the whole group or in pairs/threes.)

3. Congratulating yourself: do not be afraid of pride – tell yourself how impressed others were and remember how long you waited for this moment. (This could be done as in number 2.)

4. Sharpening perceptions: focus on certain elements of the experience and block out others. This could be done in pairs with each person telling the other what he decided to focus on and what to block out and why.

5. Assimilation: allow yourself to get totally immersed in the pleasure and try not to think about other matters. This would be an appropriate self-reflecting and ending activity for a training session.

8

Summary

This chapter has used the theory of CBT and applied it to working with individual children, particularly through use of contingency contracting. Links between CBT and Positive Psychology (Peterson, 2006) are explored, especially in terms of focusing on achieving a happier life, meaningful goals and developing competencies for problem-solving; reframing negative thoughts and actions; and finding time for pleasant activities. Gardener's theory of multiple intelligences (1983) is provided as an example of how competencies might be assessed and measured.

Questions for You to Consider

- Can you think of a pupil who would benefit from a behaviour contract and think about how you might go about drawing it up and what/who might be included in the content?

- How might you go about helping children and young people to keep track of what they do in order to help you and them to identify their abilities and interests?

- How might you use activities in this chapter to help angry pupils reframe their negative thoughts and feelings?

- Think about some children recently referred to you for fighting, how might you find out if they fit in with any one or more of the seven multiple intelligences?

Writing Contracts: Identifying the Behaviours

Inappropriate Behaviours Associated with Loss of Control	Target Behaviours Related to Managing Anger
....	....
....	....
....	....
....	....
....	....
....	....
....	....

Specific behaviours needed to reach target behaviour:

....

....

....

....

Writing Contracts: Reinforcing the Behaviours

Teaching behaviours to reinforce the target behaviour:

....

....

....

....

Rewards that could be Used	Consequences that could be Applied
....	....
....	....
....	....
....	....
....	....

Bonuses for pupil meeting all of the desired behaviours:

....

....

....

Chapter 9: PowerPoint Presentations: Anger Management and Conflict Resolution Training for School Staff

Introduction

There are two PowerPoint sessions for staff training. The facilitator notes accompanying the slides contains advice and ideas for facilitators to use when delivering the presentations. As general guidance it would be more preferable not to give out the 'handouts' version of this presentation until the end of the session.

Session 1 can be delivered separately from Session 2 which can be delivered as a 90 minute twilight session. Staff attending the second session must also have previously attended the first session.

Alternatively, Sessions 1 and 2 can be combined and delivered as a half-day INSET for staff. The purpose of both sessions is to raise staff awareness of anger and conflict, for themselves as adults and for them to use their understanding to help children and young people.

The overall aim of the staff training is to raise general awareness of anger management and conflict resolution issues. The training is also useful preparation for any staff involved in running anger management groups in school, described in Chapters 6 and 7. Chapter 7 describes more fully how a series of hourly sessions for groups of 6-8 pupils over a term might be delivered.

The PowerPoint sessions should be used as a general introduction to 'anger' whilst the activities in the book provide a more specific investigation of anger and how to respond effectively. The book provides a framework around which to create an effective whole-school policy.

The aims of Session 1 are to:

- consider what is meant by anger and conflict
- introduce the firework model
- explain some possible causes of conflict and look at how we might respond
- explore some practical ways to manage anger.

The aims of Session 2 are to:

- introduce the storm metaphor as a compliment to the firework model
- use the assault cycle as a means of weathering storms.

In both sessions various activities are provided. As the training is related to the various chapters in the book it is expected that the facilitator will have read the relevant text. The facilitator can extend the training by supplementing this content with either activities taken from the relevant chapter or suitable new activities.

9

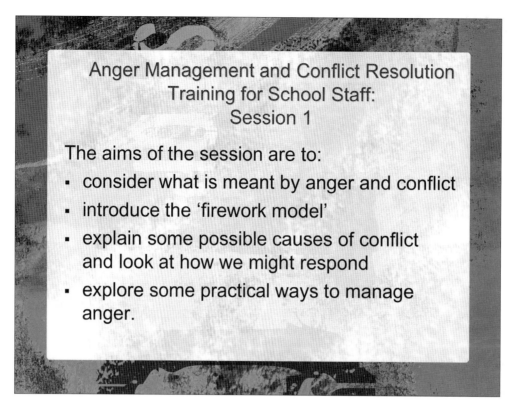

Anger Management and Conflict Resolution
Training for School Staff:
Session 1

The aims of the session are to:

- consider what is meant by anger and conflict
- introduce the 'firework model'
- explain some possible causes of conflict and look at how we might respond
- explore some practical ways to manage anger.

Facilitator Notes for Slide 1

What is meant by anger and conflict is covered at the beginning of Chapter 1.

The firework model and storm metaphor are introduced at the beginning of Chapter 4. The storm metaphor will be introduced in Session 2 to help recap on the firework model as well as to reinforce the concept.

The description of conflict resolution in Chapter 1 provides a detailed explanation of some of the possible causes of conflict. 'How do you respond to conflict?' is the first activity at the end of the chapter.

There is a general description of anger management in Chapter 1 with some practical suggestions for staff.

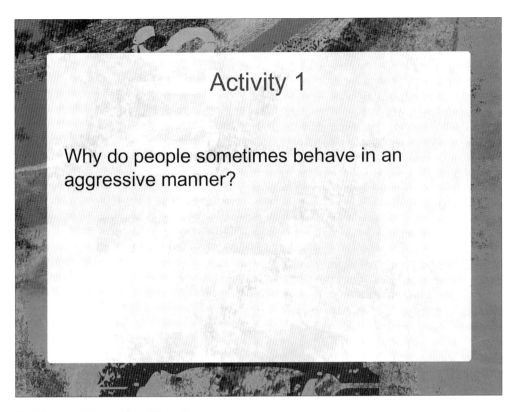

Activity 1

Why do people sometimes behave in an aggressive manner?

Facilitator Notes for Slide 2

Ask the group to work in small groups of up to six people to answer the question: 'Why do people sometimes behave in an aggressive manner?'

Take feedback from each of the small groups and first see if answers can be grouped into themes in some way especially where the responses are quite similar. Obtain consensus from the whole group. The aim is to see how these themes might fit with the content of Slide 3 (see below).

An example of:

- *Extreme displeasure* might be on someone making sexist comments.
- An *instinctive feeling* might be based on an 'aggressive tone' of voice.
- A secondary emotion might be based on someone's appearance.
- A *reflection of emotional difficulties* might be related to judgements about particular conditions, say ADHD.
- A *useful emotion* might be getting angry over the misuse of power in a relationship.

9

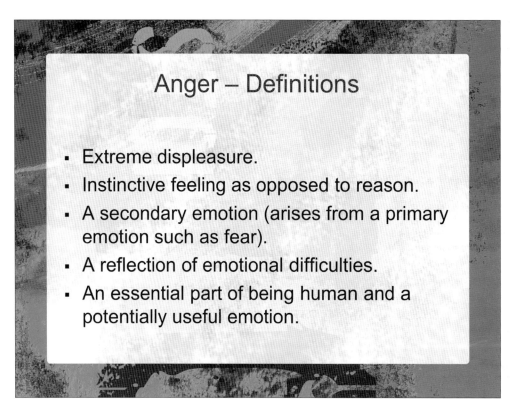

Facilitator Notes for Slide 3

Discuss the content of this slide with the themes produced by staff working in their small groups (Activity 1) and note the description of anger in Chapter 1.

The above definitions suggest that:

- anger can be described as extreme annoyance disapproval, discomfort, discontent, disgust, dissatisfaction, offense, resentment and unhappiness

- anger can be prompted by impulse or simply be a natural tendency in particular situations

- anger may not be the only emotion displayed

- anger may be part of an ongoing problem

- anger is a natural and essential part of being a human being: it is ok to be angry in   certain situations (for example, when an older child is bullying a younger or vulnerable child). The key issue is how that anger is displayed and acted upon.

Note: If children misinterpret an adult's extreme displeasure, instinctive feelings, secondary emotions or judgements about their difficulties then this can be perceived by children as expressions of rejection.

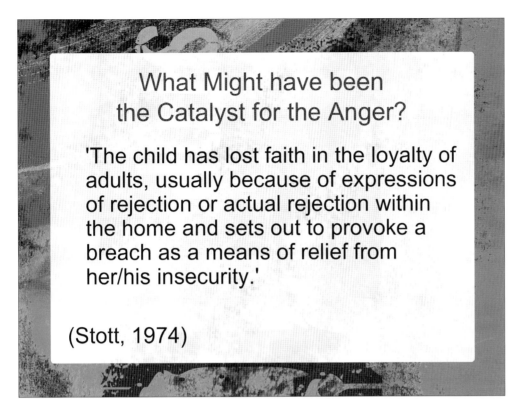

Facilitator Notes for Slide 4

The quote above is a definition of 'hostility' taken from the Bristol Social Adjustment Guide. Hostility takes two forms:

1. Provocative acts calculated to make the child an outcast.

2. A sullen avoidance of offers of friendship.

Activity 2 – So What is the Challenge?

Ask staff to work in small groups of up to six people again: you can keep the groups the same as for Activity 1 or you can mix them up. Ask the small groups to list any challenges for them and their pupils regarding anger management and conflict resolution.

Take feedback and record this on a flipchart.

Compare the small group response with Slide 5.

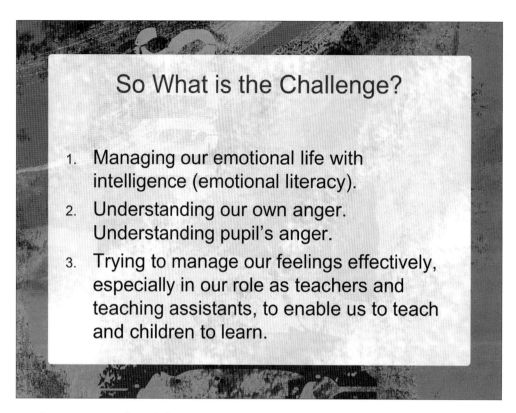

So What is the Challenge?

1. Managing our emotional life with intelligence (emotional literacy).

2. Understanding our own anger. Understanding pupil's anger.

3. Trying to manage our feelings effectively, especially in our role as teachers and teaching assistants, to enable us to teach and children to learn.

Facilitator Notes for Slide 5

1. Emotional literacy is the ability to manage yourself and your own emotions and to understand what other people are thinking and feeling. Most political leaders are past masters at these techniques. Their stage skills are excellent, they can strike just the right note of concern, humour, toughness or tenderness depending on the situation. When they get it wrong we can be both shocked and concerned. We expect our leaders to be faultless in these areas.

2. Reframe the definition of emotional literacy to the emotion of anger in particular.

3. Encompasses the wider definition of emotional literacy in the context of teaching and learning.

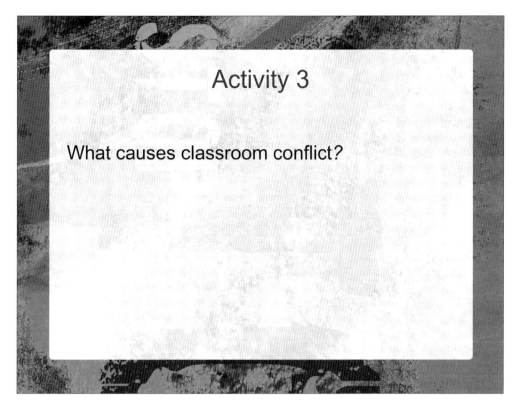

Activity 3

What causes classroom conflict?

Facilitator Notes for Slide 6

Ask the group to work in small groups of up to six people to answer the question: 'What causes classroom conflict?'

Take feedback from each of the small groups and first see if answers can be grouped in some way, especially where the responses are quite similar. Obtain consensus from the whole group and then see if these groups of answers can be put into themes to cover:

- Competitive atmosphere.
- Intolerant atmosphere.
- Poor communication.
- Inappropriate expression of emotions.
- Lack of conflict resolution skills.
- Misuse of power by the teacher.

Note: A more detailed description of the above themes can be found in Chapter 1.

9

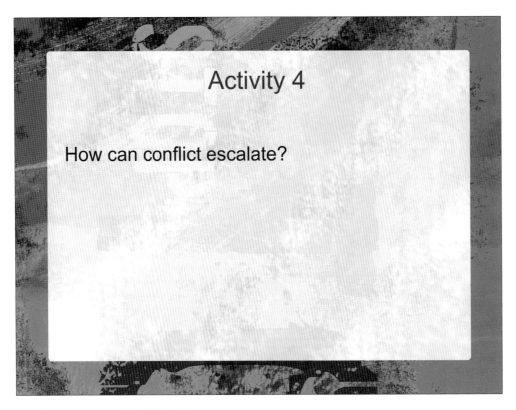

Activity 4

How can conflict escalate?

Facilitator Notes for Slide 7

Ask the group to work in small groups of up to six people to answer the question: 'How can conflict escalate?'

Take feedback from each of the small groups and first see if answers can be grouped in some way, especially where the responses are quite similar. Obtain consensus from the whole group and see if the grouped responses fit into the any one or more of the following list:

- There's an increase in exposed emotion (for example, anger, frustration).
- There's an increase in perceived threat.
- More people get involved and take sides.
- The pupils were not friends prior to the conflict.
- The pupils involved in the conflict have few peacemaking skills at their disposal.

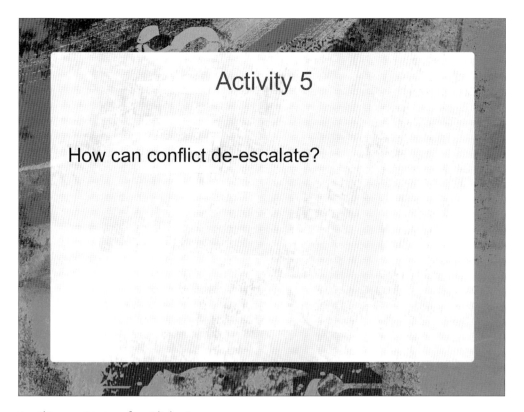

Activity 5

How can conflict de-escalate?

Facilitator Notes for Slide 8

Ask the group to work in small groups of up to six people to answer the question: 'How can conflict de-escalate?'

Take feedback from each of the small groups and first see if answers can be grouped in some way especially where the responses are quite similar. Obtain consensus from the whole group and see if the grouped responses fit into the any one or more of the following list:

- If attention is focused on the problem and not the participants.
- If there's a decrease in exposed emotion and threat.
- The pupils were friends prior to the conflict.

The pupils know how to come up with peaceful solutions or have someone to   help them.

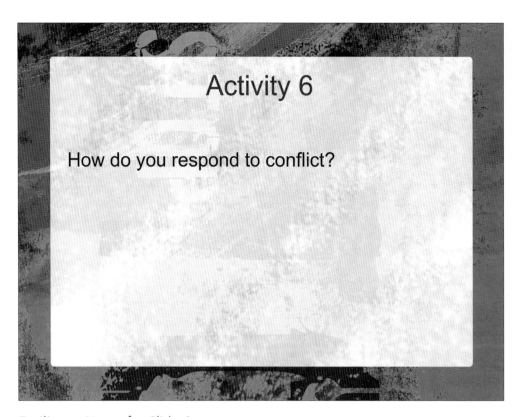

Activity 6

How do you respond to conflict?

Facilitator Notes for Slide 9

Ask the staff to individually complete the, 'How Do You Respond to Conflict?' questionnaire. Their scores should be totalled under each of the five columns. The descriptions of these columns are given on Slide 10.

Note that this activity appears as the first activity at the end of Chapter 1 and can be printed from the CD-ROM.

How do You Respond to Conflict?

1. The no-nonsense approach.

2. The problem-solving approach.

3. The compromising approach.

4. The smoothing approach.

5. The ignoring approach.

Facilitator Notes for Slide 10

Ask the group to discuss the findings from their completed questionnaires (Activity 6) with a follow-up question for them to answer in their pairs (that is, each one of a pair should ask the other person) why they think they responded to the questionnaire in the way they did.

Take feedback and comment on any similarities and differences between the pairs. Think about what this might mean for the overall school behaviour policy.

9

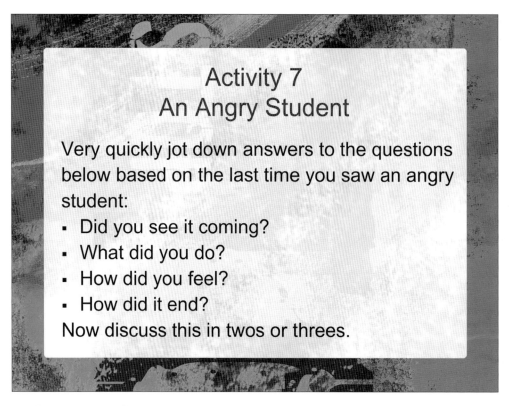

Activity 7
An Angry Student

Very quickly jot down answers to the questions below based on the last time you saw an angry student:

- Did you see it coming?
- What did you do?
- How did you feel?
- How did it end?

Now discuss this in twos or threes.

Facilitator Notes for Slide 11

This activity acts as an introduction to the Firework Model on Slide 12. There are three components to the firework model:

1. Trigger.

2. Fuse.

3. Explosive firework.

The trigger is the match that lights the firework and sets off the anger response. The body of the firework is our reaction internally and externally to the event outside us, and the fuse is the mind or our thoughts about the event. There are external factors and internal factors which contribute to the explosion. The external factors we may or may not have control over for example, stress in the classroom – too hot, too many people, someone pushing into you. The internal factors we can control. These are our thoughts, which stem from a belief we hold. The other internal factor we can control is our physical reaction to a situation. How we interpret the event can make us angry or calm us down. Our internal response stems from our beliefs and expectations in certain situations, which triggers the internal dialogue we have in our own heads. So you should take feedback and think of the groups' answers in terms of:

- Seeing it coming being the 'trigger'.

- What they did and how they felt as the 'fuse'.

- How it ended as the 'explosion'.

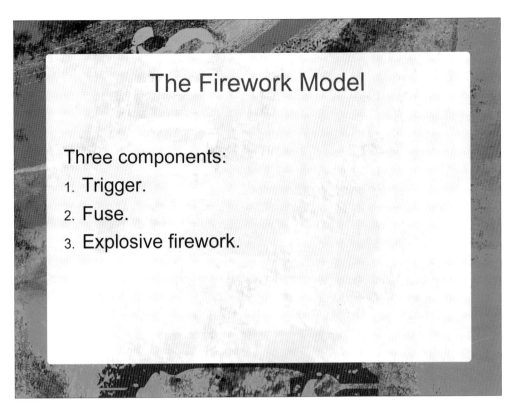

The Firework Model

Three components:
1. Trigger.
2. Fuse.
3. Explosive firework.

Facilitator Notes for Slide 12

This has been adapted from Novaco's Model for Anger Arousal (1975) and has proven particularly accessible and memorable to pupils during anger management groups. For example, grasping the notion of avoiding triggers, such as people, situations, times, words, or else minimising or reducing their impact by being able to rethink or reframe their reaction to triggers and lengthen their fuse or extinguish it before explosion!

1. The match ignites the fuse and this leads to thoughts and feelings.

2. Is the mind reacting and causing thoughts and feelings (for example, fear or threat).

3. The cylinder is the body responding physiologically and may lead to anger.

The trigger can be any of our five senses, person or situation specific and can be on any scale of severity. The fuse can be thoughts and feelings and these may or may not power up our anger. The fuse may be short or long and it can sometimes be cut or extinguished. The firework is the explosion which may be minor or devastating. Containment can reduce the impact on others and, it is often advisable to remove other children if the explosion is too dangerous.

9

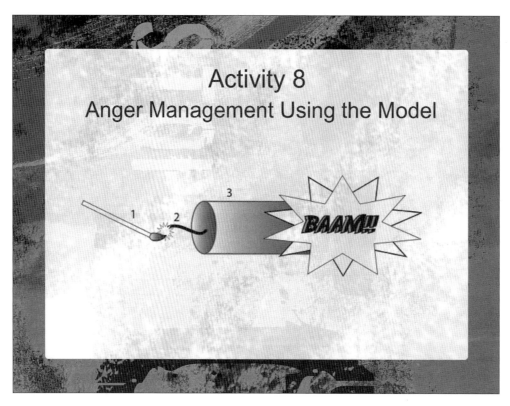

Facilitator Notes for Slide 13

The activity page 'How the Firework Model Applies to Me When I Get Angry' at end of Chapter 4 can be used here to illustrate the diagram above for staff. The activity page can be printed from the CD-ROM.

Staff should complete the activity individually and then discuss their responses in pairs. Take a sample of feedback from some of the pairs to get a flavour of their responses.

You can compare staff responses to each of the components of the firework model with their response to Activity 8.

Activity 9
Tactics for Individual Pupils

- Quickly jot down any 'tactics' you currently use to help manage anger effectively.
- Discuss these tactics in twos or threes.

Facilitator Notes for Slide 14

You are going to compare the staff responses with the points on Slide 15.

You can also make reference to the:

- need for whole-school approaches in general (Chapter 2) to compliment   and support individual tactics

- teacher skills necessary to implement a whole-school approach to anger management (Chapter 3) apply equally to individual tactics.

Tactics for Individual Interventions

- Using self-talk/'I' statements: 'I can hack this, I've been here before.'
- Self-calming, for example, trigger word or action.
- Relaxation, taking exercise or engaging in some form of physical activity.
- Negotiation and use of behaviour contracts.
- Using problem-solving techniques.
- Using solution focused techniques.
- Accentuating the positive.
- Use of peer mediation.

Facilitator Notes for Slide 15

Self-talk/'I' statements; self-calming; relaxation and taking exercise are covered in Chapter 5.

The use of behaviour contracts is covered in Chapter 8.

Problem-solving and solution-focused techniques are illustrated in Chapter 4.

Accentuating the positive is included within Chapter 8.

Peer mediation can be used along the lines of the problem-solving activities described in Chapter 1, whereby children and young people are trained to 'mediate' between peers in conflict by applying problem-solving techniques with their peers who are in conflict with each other.

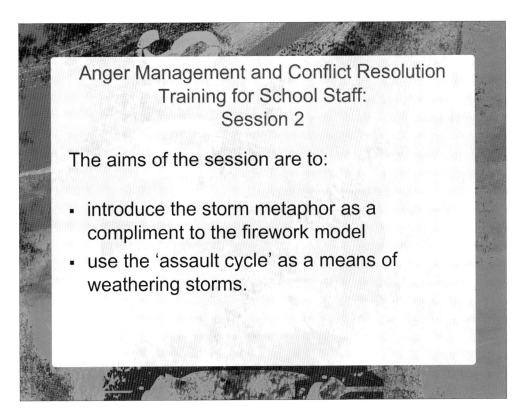

Anger Management and Conflict Resolution
Training for School Staff:
Session 2

The aims of the session are to:

- introduce the storm metaphor as a
  compliment to the firework model
- use the 'assault cycle' as a means of
  weathering storms.

Facilitator Notes for Slide 16

The storm metaphor is associated with the Educational Psychologist Peter Sharp who first suggested that anger is like a storm: storms happen and they do not ask for permission.

Sometimes you get a warning such as gathering clouds, changes in air pressure or wind direction, light fading or sudden darkness. And so it is with some angry outbursts or violent incidents. Avoidance strategies can help in trying to head off a storm or to go round it rather than through it.

9

Facilitator Notes for Slide 17

If the Firework Model is a schematic representation at the individual level, showing what happens when children get angry, then the metaphor of 'a storm' may help to describe anger in terms of the 'bigger picture' where environmental influences are as important as the reaction of the individual child. The 'storm metaphor' is described in Chapter 4.

Metaphors intend to suggest, and reveal, certain images that enable us to see a likeness between initially different events and metaphors gives us two ideas for one.

Metaphors do not add facts to a description; rather, they add depth of meaning to the nature of a phenomenon or experience. They provide a model of novel ways of looking at behaviour or thinking about a topic. They simplify events in the terms of a schema, or concept, that emphasises some properties more than others. They give communications an intimate or personal quality because of the concrete referents of metaphorical imagery.

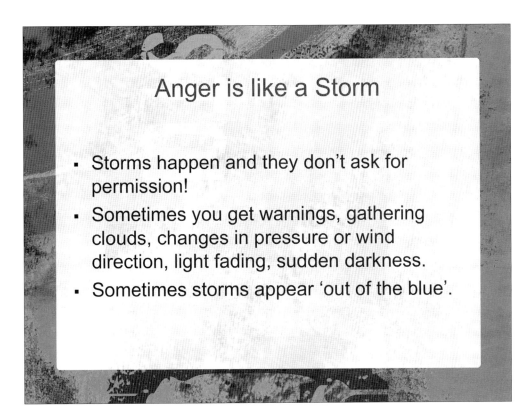

Anger is like a Storm

- Storms happen and they don't ask for permission!
- Sometimes you get warnings, gathering clouds, changes in pressure or wind direction, light fading, sudden darkness.
- Sometimes storms appear 'out of the blue'.

Facilitator Notes for Slide 18

Storms occur and will go on occurring but there are ways to avoid storms or to minimise their impact – to weather them and deal with any aftermath.

Some storms are heralded by well-understood indicators such as gathering clouds and changes in pressure or wind direction, fading light or sudden darkness – so it is with some angry outbursts or violent incidents. Avoidance strategies can help in trying to head off a storm or go round it rather than through it.

Some storms appear 'unannounced' and both teachers and parents will sometimes describe children's anger as appearing 'out of the blue'. Weathering the storm – defusing anger at point of difficulty and before anger becomes dangerous.

Storms are inevitable – even where strategies have been tried, so strategies for clearing up after the storm – learning from experience and planning to reduce likelihood of a similar storm are needed.

9

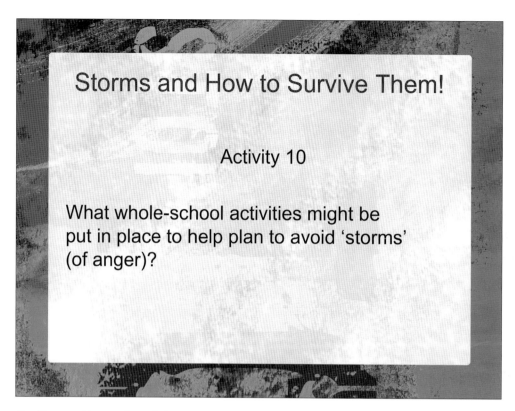

Storms and How to Survive Them!

Activity 10

What whole-school activities might be
put in place to help plan to avoid 'storms'
(of anger)?

Facilitator Notes for Slide 19

Staff should work in groups of up to six people to answer the question: What whole-school activities might be put in place to help plan to avoid 'storms' (of anger)?

Take feedback from each group and see if you can collapse the responses into a collective agreed revised list of activities.

Ask the groups to categorise the revised list and compare their categories with the content of Slide 20.

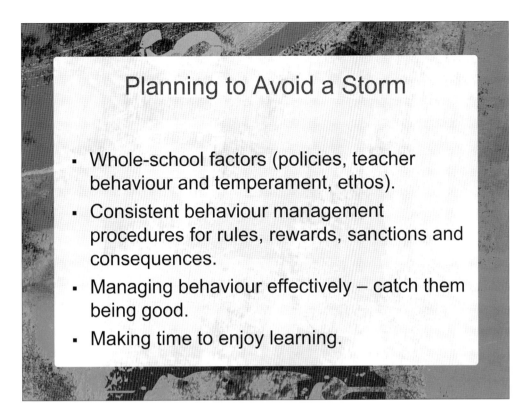

Planning to Avoid a Storm

- Whole-school factors (policies, teacher behaviour and temperament, ethos).
- Consistent behaviour management procedures for rules, rewards, sanctions and consequences.
- Managing behaviour effectively – catch them being good.
- Making time to enjoy learning.

Facilitator Notes for Slide 20

Planning to avoid storms is described in more detail in Chapter 4 and covers the need for:

- Strong leadership – identifying anger management as priority component of behaviour policy.

- Consistency of practice between and amongst staff.

- Good atmosphere – shared values (cohesiveness) and attractive environment.

- High expectations of behaviour and achievement.

- Constancy – classroom environments relatively predictable with gradual/evolutionary change.

- Clear focus on teaching and learning anger management strategies – reduce competition and confrontation.

- Pupil incentives to succeed and share responsibility for learning and participation in life of school.

- Parental involvement.

- Extracurricular activities.

9

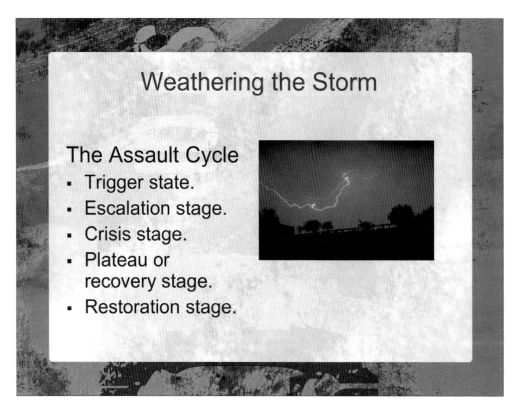

Facilitator Notes for Slide 21

Trigger – related to firework model – 'ignites' child's fuse, stimulating thoughts and feelings leading to anger (for example, threats to self-esteem/image; personal safety; property).

Escalation – body preparing 'physiologically' for fight or flight, adrenaline rush; muscles tense; rapid breathing; raised blood pressure (shortening of firework fuse).

Crisis – child unable to make rational judgements or demonstrate empathy with others (firework exploding).

Plateau/recovery – anger begins to subside and it takes time for the body to return to normal: it's easy to escalate anger again by intervening inappropriately as body is still partly prepared for action and there are feelings of vulnerability and confusion at this stage.

Restoration – the body needs to rest and recover from high arousal state: the ability to listen and think clearly begins to return and the child may begin to feel guilty.

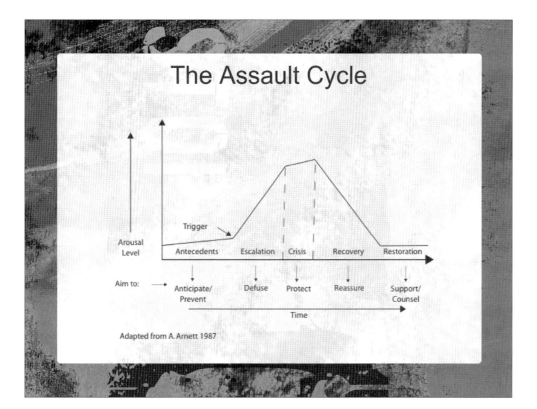

Facilitator Notes for Slide 22

The **antecedents/trigger phase** is related to the firework model in which a child's fuse may be ignited, stimulating thoughts and feelings which can lead to displays of anger as a result of, for example, threats to self-esteem or self-image and threats to personal safety or property.

The **escalation phase** is when the body is preparing 'physiologically' for a 'fight or flight' response: there is usually an adrenaline rush, muscles tense with rapid breathing and raised blood pressure. It equates with a shortening of the firework fuse.

The **crisis phase** is where the child is unable to make rational judgements or is unable to demonstrate empathy with others. This is when the firework is exploding.

The **plateau or recovery phase** is where the child's anger begins to subside. It usually takes time for the body to return to normal and it is easy for the anger to escalate again if there is an inappropriate adult intervention because the child's body is still partly prepared for action and the child is likely to be feeling particularly vulnerable and confused at this stage.

The **restoration phase** is where the child's body needs to rest and recover from its high state of arousal. It is usually the stage at which the child is able to listen and think clearly. The child may then begin to feel guilty.

The early warning signs for the onset of the cycle can begin with physical agitation such as pacing up and down, fiddling with equipment and twitching legs. A change in facial expression, eye contact, body posture, tone of voice, position in the classroom accompanied by rapid mood swings is likely. Children may go through this cycle in a matter of minutes, hours, days or weeks.

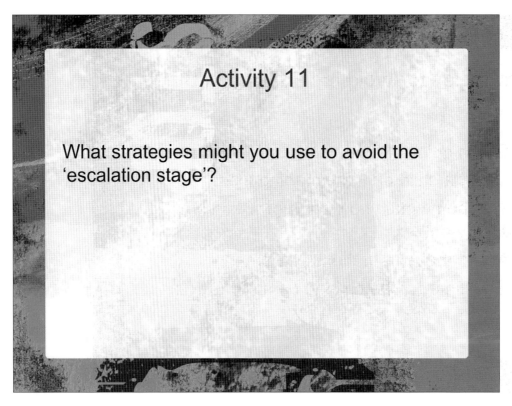

Activity 11

What strategies might you use to avoid the 'escalation stage'?

Facilitator Notes for Slide 23

Have the staff work in their same groups of up to six people or move them around so that they are working in different groups.

Ask the groups to answer the question: What strategies might you use to avoid the 'escalation stage'?

Take feedback and record on a flipchart to compare their responses with Slide 24.

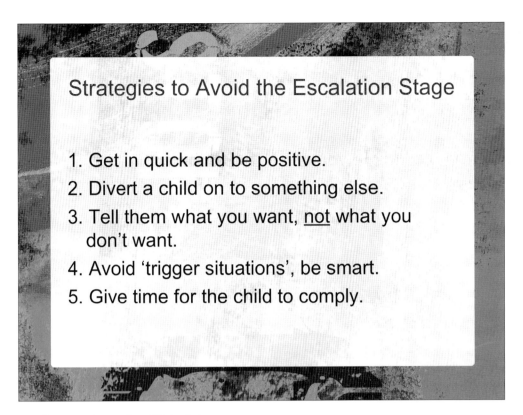

Strategies to Avoid the Escalation Stage

1. Get in quick and be positive.
2. Divert a child on to something else.
3. Tell them what you want, <u>not</u> what you don't want.
4. Avoid 'trigger situations', be smart.
5. Give time for the child to comply.

Facilitator Notes for Slide 24

You will want to use examples from Activity 11 to illustrate the points above.

9

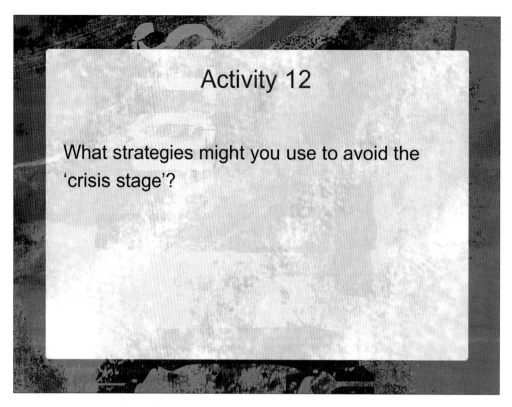

Activity 12

What strategies might you use to avoid the 'crisis stage'?

Facilitator Notes for Slide 25

Have the staff work in their same groups of up to six people or move them around so that they are working in different groups.

Ask the groups to answer the question: What strategies might you use to avoid the 'crisis stage'?

Take feedback and record on a flipchart to compare their responses with Slide 26.

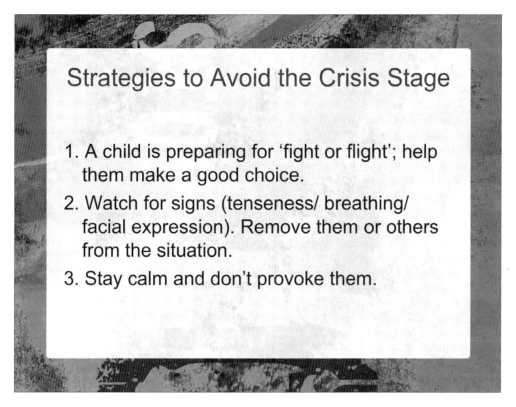

Strategies to Avoid the Crisis Stage

1. A child is preparing for 'fight or flight'; help them make a good choice.
2. Watch for signs (tenseness/ breathing/ facial expression). Remove them or others from the situation.
3. Stay calm and don't provoke them.

Facilitator Notes for Slide 26

You will want to compare staff responses with the content of this slide. It's worth you commenting on the first point as follows:

1. 'Fight of flight' is the body's response to perceived threat or danger. During this reaction, certain hormones like adrenalin and cortisol are released, speeding the heart rate, slowing digestion, shunting blood flow to major muscle groups, and changing various other autonomic nervous functions giving the body a burst of energy and strength. Originally named for its ability to enable us to physically fight or run away when faced with danger.

2. Very often children are unaware of their body reactions when they get angry.

3. You might want to ask staff what strategies they successfully use when faced with an angry child and what comments they have found to provoke children further such that they get even more angry.

9

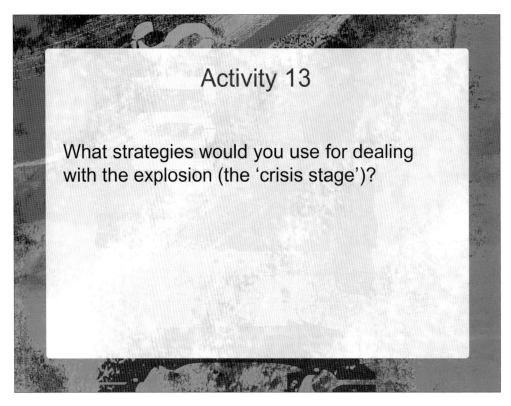

Activity 13

What strategies would you use for dealing
with the explosion (the 'crisis stage')?

Facilitator Notes for Slide 27

Have the staff work in their same groups of up to six people or move them around so that
they are working in different groups.

Ask the groups to answer the question: What strategies might you use for dealing with the
'crisis stage'?

Take feedback and record on a flipchart to compare their responses with Slide 28.

The Crisis Stage (Explosion)

- Make things safe, remove dangerous objects and get others to leave.
- Use physical restraint only if the child is a danger to themselves or others.
- Stay in control and do not make it worse (by imitation/ridicule and so on).
- Get help. Don't be proud, be smart.

Facilitator Notes for Slide 28

You will want to compare the staff responses to Activity 13 with the content of this slide.

You will want to discuss the following:

- What arrangements will need to be in place to enable other pupils to leave the room?
- What are the school and local authority policies on restraint?
- What kinds of staff comments might make the situation worse?
- What kinds of things can staff do to stay in control of the situation?
- Who might they get help from and how might this help be accessed?

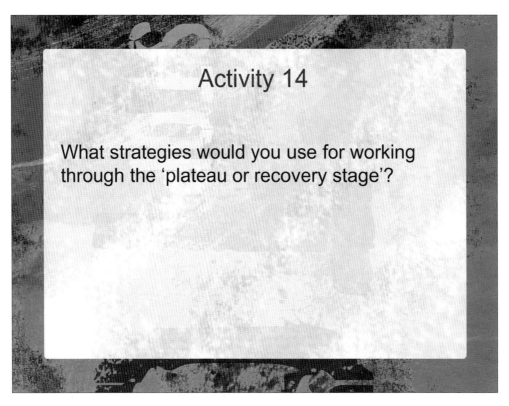

Activity 14

What strategies would you use for working through the 'plateau or recovery stage'?

Facilitator Notes for Slide 29

Have the staff work in their same groups of up to six people or move them around so that they are working in different groups.

Ask the groups to answer the question: What strategies might be used for working through the 'plateau or recovery stage'?

Take feedback and record on a flipchart to compare their responses with Slide 30.

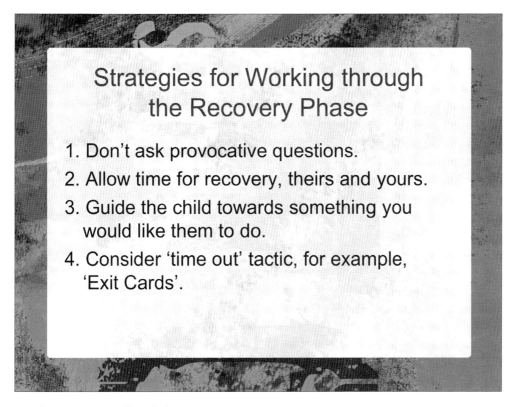

Strategies for Working through
the Recovery Phase

1. Don't ask provocative questions.
2. Allow time for recovery, theirs and yours.
3. Guide the child towards something you would like them to do.
4. Consider 'time out' tactic, for example, 'Exit Cards'.

Facilitator Notes for Slide 30

You will want to compare staff responses to Activity 14 with the content of this slide.

You can ask the group for:

- examples of provocative questions to avoid, and these might include: 'Why did you just do that?' 'I thought you were more mature than that?' 'Only babies have temper tantrums?'

- their views on the length of recovery time

- examples of activities children have chosen to do during this stage   as these could be offered to children as part of a menu of activities   to use during recovery time

- examples of other 'time out' tactics.

Getting Beyond Restoration Stage

1. Don't try to load the child up with more guilt.
2. If there was anything positive to praise then go for it, for example, well done for avoiding hitting.
3. Discuss how to change the behaviour in the future, in a positive and caring way, for example, 'If you feel that angry again, use your exit card.'

Facilitator Notes for Slide 31

1. You can ask the whole staff group to 'brainstorm' some ideas for avoiding loading up a child with more guilt and these might include, for example, 'You know you really did hurt Darren,' 'You have made a real mess of the display that the class made.'

2. Saying 'well done' for an aggressive behaviour that did not occur during the outburst can be a very positive feature at this stage and it also helps prevent loading the child with more guilt.

3. This is about reminding the child that there are systems in place at school that can help prevent the crisis stage. This means discussing with the child when during the escalation stage he should consider making use of such systems. The child may need to be taught how to use the system especially when in a somewhat heightened state of arousal during the escalation stage.

Conclude these awareness raising sessions with mention of the more detailed and specific activities contained in the book which staff may wish to refer to.

Chapter 10: **Conclusion**

The rationale for adopting a CBT approach to anger management is because CBT is based on the idea that pupils' 'thoughts' cause their feelings and influence their resultant actions and behaviours, rather than external things, like teachers, and situations and events in the classroom, playground and corridors and so on. This means that as managers we can encourage teachers to change the ways their pupils think so that pupils feel or act better even if the situation in the classroom, playground or corridor does not change.

The firework model and storm metaphor (Chapter 4) are good examples of explaining to teachers and pupils how their thoughts and feelings determine how they will act once an angry thought has been triggered. The firework model has helped pupils think about avoiding triggers such as certain people, situations, times or words, or else minimising or reducing their impact by rethinking or reframing reactions to triggers.

The storm metaphor helps describe anger in terms of the 'bigger picture' in which the importance of environmental influences is considered as well as the pupil's reaction. Included within the storm metaphor analogy are solution-orientated approaches that focus on children's strengths and how they would prefer things to be other than being 'stormy'. Action-planning and goal-setting are arrived at by 'scaling' the future direction starting from how things are at the moment.

Taking a CBT approach does not mean that we should tell teachers and pupils how they should feel. However, most young people either seeking or agreeing to help do not want to feel the way they have been feeling, especially if their inability to control their anger has had dire consequences, such as getting excluded from school. Teachers seeking ways of managing, possibly their own as well as pupils' anger, may also not want to feel the way they have been feeling about themselves and their pupils. The PowerPoint presentation aims to raise staff awareness of anger and conflict, for themselves as adults, and for them to use their understanding of anger and conflict to help children and young people.

Visual imagery, relaxation and role-play (Chapter 5), another CBT approach, enable pupils to explore both what it feels like to be angry and relaxed in a safe and controlled manner. Relaxation training is an essential part of anger management and Chapter 5 shows staff how to develop activities to help children relax. Role-play activities enable children to understand how conflict can arise and then to explore the possible alternatives for diffusing and resolving such situations.

The anger management intervention programme (Chapter 7) provides opportunities for pupils to make sense of the overwhelming problems that can occur in school by breaking them down into a sequence of thoughts, emotions, physical feelings and actions. This makes it easier for pupils to see how their thoughts, emotions, feelings and actions are connected especially in difficult or problematic situations.

This approach can help pupils to break a vicious cycle of unpleasant or unrealistic thinking about themselves because when they learn to see the parts of the sequence clearly they can change them and therefore change the way they feel. The intended outcome of the anger management intervention programme is to help pupils participating in this kind of group work to get to a point where they work out their own ways of tackling problems without getting angry and losing their temper.

CBT is based on a philosophy that it teaches the benefits of feeling 'calm' when confronted with undesirable situations. The approach also emphasises the fact that angry young people will be faced with undesirable situations whether they get upset about them or not. If they do get upset about their problems, then they have two problems: the problem itself and their upset about the problem. One type of CBT approach for helping children with the problem and their upset is the use of 'contingency contracting' (Chapter 8) which is aimed at helping both pupils and teachers to bring about the greatest relative advantage or the least relative disadvantage in dealing with the problem in a given situation. Problem-solving and conflict resolution techniques for teachers in general are described in Chapter 1 where activities are designed to check out the degree of consistency amongst staff in responses to conflict as part of a whole-school approach to anger management.

Most young people probably want to have the fewest number of problems possible. So when they are able to learn how to more calmly accept a personal problem, not only are they likely to feel better, but it should also enable them to be in a better position to make use of their multiple intelligences, knowledge, energy and resources to resolve the problem. Positive Psychology (Chapter 8) seeks to adopt preventative measures by suggesting that positive interpersonal qualities should be systematically identified and built upon for each pupil. This approach also focuses on developing competencies for problem-solving that include a consideration of Gardener's (1983) seven multiple intelligences for both teaching and learning as well as encouraging young people to capitalise on their own interests and abilities.

CBT focuses on the young people's goals, be it through contingency contracting or Positive Psychology. We do not really want to encourage staff to tell young people what their goals 'should' be or what they 'should' tolerate. We should inspire staff to be, rather, directive in the sense that they show young people how to think and behave in ways to obtain what they want, especially if they can direct pupils towards alternative ways of dealing with conflict. As managers promoting teachers to use CBT approaches, we are suggesting that our staff do not tell young people 'what' to do but rather, teach young people 'how' to (do), as when implementing an anger management group for them (Chapter 7). As managers we should be asking teachers to galvanise young people to practise the techniques learned through individual or group intervention programmes so that young people really are successful in managing their anger.

CBT is based on the scientifically supported assumption that most emotional and behavioural reactions such as temper tantrums are learned and Chapter 1 makes clear the distinction between anger and conflict in this respect. Therefore, the goal of any individual or group intervention is to help young people to 'unlearn' their unwanted reactions (inappropriate expressions of anger) and to learn a new way of reacting such as talking through situations calmly. However, these methods have nothing to do with 'just talking'. People can 'just talk' with anyone. The educational emphasis of CBT has an additional benefit in that it can lead to long-term results.

When young people understand how and why they are doing well in managing their anger, they know what to do to continue doing well.

The teacher skills necessary to implement a whole-school approach to anger management (Chapter 3) are built on the CBT approaches, by outlining teacher and pupil responsibilities within the 4Rs framework and acknowledging the importance of recognising the factors that affect the classroom dynamics and the different types of learners. In a whole-school approach to anger management (Chapter 2) the importance for staff of understanding anger, how it is expressed and the ways of managing their own and pupil's anger is strongly emphasised. Not only is the need for an anger management strategy highlighted but also the need to consider practices that have a sound research base and proven record of success and CBT approaches fit the bill in these respects!

Bibliography

Ainscow, M., Farrell, P., Tweddle, D. & Malkki, G. (1999) *The role of LEAs in developing inclusive policies and practices*, British Journal of Special Education 26 (3): 136-40.

Albert, L. (2003) *Cooperative Discipline*. Circle Pines, MN: American Guidance Service.

Audit Commission (2002) *Special Educational Needs*: a mainstream issue. London.

Ayers, H., Clarke, D. & Ross, A. (1996) *Assessing Individual Needs*. London: David Fulton Publishers.

Bernard, B. (1991) *Fostering Resiliency in Kids: Protective factors in the family, school and community*. San Francisco, CA: Montana Office of Public Instruction and the Montana Board of Crime Control.

Bernard, B. (2004) *Resiliency: What we have learned*. San Francisco: West Ed.

Bodine, R. J. & Crawford, D. K. (Eds.) (1998) *The Handbook of Conflict Resolution Education: A guide to building quality programs in schools*. San Francisco: Jossey-Bass.

Bodine, R. J., Crawford, D. K. & Schrumf, F. (2003) *Creating the Peaceable School: Program Guide: A comprehensive program for teaching conflict resolution. 2nd Edition*. Champaign, Illanois: Research Press Publishers.

Bowkett, S. (1999) *Self-Intelligence: A Handbook for Developing Confidence, Self-Esteem and Interpersonal Skills*. Stafford: Network Educational Press Ltd.

Bryant, F. B. (2003) Savouring Beliefs Inventory (SBI): 'A scale for measuring beliefs about savouring'. *Journal of Mental Health*, 12, 175-196.

Clarke, G. N., Pohde, P., Lewinsohn, P. M., Hops, H., Seeley, J. R. (1999) 'Cognitive behavioural treatment of adolescent depression: Efficacy of acute group treatments and booster session'. *Journal of American Academy of Child Adolescent Psychiatry*, 38, 272-279.

Coldwell, M., Stephenson, K., Fathallah-Caillau, I. & Coldron. J. (2003) *Evaluation of Home School Agreements*. Research Brief 455. London: DfES.

Cole, T., Visser, J. & Upton, G. (1998) *Effective Schooling for Pupils with Emotional and Behavioural Difficulties*. London: David Fulton Publishers.

Cole, T., Daniels, H. & Visser, J. (1999) *Patterns of educational provision maintained by Local Education Authorities for pupils with behaviour problems*. Report sponsored by Nuffield Foundation (Birmingham, University of Birmingham).

Cowan, D., Palomares, S. & Schilling, D. (1992) *Teaching the Skills of Conflict Resolution*. Carson, C.A.: Innerchoice Publishing.

Crowther, D., Cummings, C., Dyson, A. & Millward, A. (2003) *Schools and Area Regeneration*. Bristol: The Policy Press, for JRF.

DES (1989) *Discipline in schools: Report of the Committee of Enquiry chaired by Lord Elton (The Elton Report)*. London: HMSO.

Department for Children, School and Families (2003/4) *Permanent and Fixed Term Exclusions from Schools and Exclusion Appeals in England*. National Statistics.

DfES (2004) Working Together – *Giving Children and Young People a Say: Guidance for Head Teachers, Chairs of Governors*, LEA's, Parents, Pupils, Teachers. London: HMSO.

DfES (2004) *Removing Barriers to Achievement: The Government Strategy for SEN*. London: HMSO.

DfES (2004) *The Behaviour Improvement Programme (BIP): National Behaviour Training Curriculum Pilot Materials*. London: HMSO.

Desforges, C. with Abouchaar, A. (2003) *The impact of parental involvement, parental support and family education on pupil achievement and adjustment. A literature review*. DfES Research Report 433. London: Department for Education and Skills.

DOH and DfES (2004) *Promoting Emotional Health and Wellbeing through the National Healthy School Standard*. London: HMSO.

Earley, P., Evans, J., Collarbone, P., Gold, A. & Halpin, D. (2002) *Establishing the Current State of School Leadership In England*. London: HMSO.

Ehrenwald, J. (1991) *The History of Psychotherapy*. Northvale: Jason Aronson.

Ellenberger, H. (1970) *The Discovery of the Unconscious*. New York: Basic Books.

Farrell, P. & Tsakalidu, K. (1999) *Recent trends in the re-integration of pupils with emotional and behavioural difficulties in the United Kingdom*. School Psychology International 20 (3): 75-89.

Faupel, A., Herrick, E. & Sharp, P. (1998) *Anger Management: A Practical Guide*. London: David Fulton Publishers.

Feindler, E. L. & Ecton, R. B. (1986) *Adolescent Anger Control: Cognitive behavioural techniques*. New York: Pergamon Press.

Fitzsimmons, M. K. (1998) *School-wide Behaviour Management Systems*. Education Resources Information Centre Digest.

Flexner (1993) Metaphors to engage and educate – from the following webpage: http://www.ep.org.au/gg/lecs/metaphors.htm

Galloway, D. & Goodwin, C. (1987) *The Education of Disturbing Children*. London: Longman.

Gardener, H. (1983) *Frames of Mind: The theory of multiple intelligences*. New York: Basic.

Gardener, H. (1991) Assessment in context. The alternative to standardised testing. In B. R. Gifford & M. C. O'Connor (Eds.), *Changing assessments: Alternative views of aptitude, achievement and instruction* (pp77-120). Boston: Kluwer.

Garmezy, N. (1983) Stressors of Childhood. In N. Garmezy & M. Rutter (Eds.) *Stress, coping and development in children* (pp. 43-84). Baltimore: Johns Hopkins University Press.

Gillham, J. E., Reivich, K. J., Jaycox, L. H. & Seligman, M. E. P. (1995) 'Prevention of depressive symptoms in schoolchildren: Two year follow-up'. *Psychological Science*, 6, 343-351.

Gillham, J. E. & Reivich, K. J. (2007) Resilience Research in Children: The Penn Resiliency Project. Penn Positive Psychology Centre. University of Pennsylvania.

Goleman, D. P. (1995) Emotional Intelligence: *Why It Can Matter More Than IQ for Character, Health and Lifelong Achievement.* New York: Bantam Books.

Graham, J. & Bowling, B. (1995) *Young People And Crime: Self reported offending among 14-25 year olds in England and Wales.* Home Office Research Study 145. London: Home Office.

Griffin, J. (1986) *Wellbeing: Its meaning, measurement and moral importance. Oxford:* Clarendon.

Grimshaw, R. & Berridge, D. (1994) *Educating Disruptive Children.* London: National Children's Bureau.

Haggerty, R. J., Sherrod, L. R., Garmezy, N. & Rutter, M. (Eds.) (1996) *Stress, Risk, and Resilience in Children and Adolescents: Processes, Mechanisms, and Interventions.* Cambridge: Cambridge University Press.

Hellaby, L. (2004) *Walking the Talk.* London: David Fulton Publishers.

Huppert, F., Baylis, N. & Keverne, B. (2005) *The Science of Wellbeing.* Oxford: Oxford University Press.

Hymans, M. (2004) *Creating a Dynamic Classroom: A programme to develop co-operative behaviour for 9-14 year olds.* Bristol: Lucky Duck Publishing.

Johnson, D. W. & Johnson, R. T. (1996) *Conflict Resolution and Peer Mediation Programs in Elementary and Secondary Schools: A Review of the Research.* Review of Educational Research, Vol. 66, No. 4, 459-506.

Kahneman, D. (1999) Objective happiness. In D. Kahneman, E. Deiner & N. Schwarz (Eds.). *Wellbeing: The foundations of hedonic psychology* (pp 3-25). New York: Russell Sage.

Karwoski, L., Garratt, G. M. & Ilardi, S. S. (2006) On the integration of cognitive behavioural therapy for depression and positive psychology. *Journal of Cognitive Psychotherapy*, 20(2), 159-170.

Kelly, G. A. (1955/1991) *The Psychology of Personal Constructs, Volumes 1 and 2.* New York: WW Norton.

Lakoff, G. & Johnson, M. (1980) *Metaphors We Live By*. Chicago: Chicago University Press.

Larsen, R. J. & Frederickson, B. L. (1999) Measurement issues in emotion research. In D. Kahneman, E. Deiner & N. Schwarz (Eds.). *Wellbeing: The foundations of hedonic psychology* (pp 40-60). New York: Russell Sage.

Linley, P.A. & Joseph, S. (2004) *Positive Psychology in Practice*. New Jersey: John Wiley & Sons Inc.

McCarthy, K. & Park, J. (1998) *Learning by Heart: The Role of Emotional Education in Raising School Achievement*. London: Calouste Gulbenkian Foundation/Brighton: Remembering Education.

McCluskey, G. (2005) 'What does discipline mean in schools now?'. *Scottish Educational Review*, Vol.37, November 2005.

Maines, B. & Robinson, G. (1992) *The No Blame Approach*. Bristol: Lucky Duck Publishing.

Maines, B. & Robinson, G. (2009) *The Support Group Method Training Pack*. London: Sage Publications.

Massey, M. S. (1998) *Early Childhood Violence Prevention*. Education Resources Information Centre Digest.

Meier, A. (1993) Toward an integrated model of competency: Linking White and Bandura. *Journal of Cognitive Psychotherapy*, 7, 35-47.

Melhuish., E., Sylva, K., Sammons, P., Siraj-Blatchford, I. & Taggart, B. (2001) *Social behavioural and cognitive development at 3-4 years in relation to family background. The effective provision of pre-school education, EPPE project*. (Technical paper 7) DfEE. London: The Institute of Education.

National Commission for Education (1996) *Success against the odds: Effective schools in disadvantaged areas*.

Nelsen, J., Escobar, L., Ortolano, K., Duffy, R. & Owen-Sohocki, D. (2001) *Positive Discipline: A Teacher's A-Z Guide*. New York: Three Rivers Press.

Novaco, R. W. (1975) *Anger Control: The development and evaluation of an experimental treatment*. Lexington, MA: Heath.

Nussbaum, M. (1992) Human functioning and social justice: In defense of Aristotelian essentialism. *Political Theory*, 20. 202-246.

Orbach, S. (1999) *Towards Emotional Literacy*. London: Virago.

Palomares, S. & Akin, T. (1995) *Managing Conflict: Strategies, activities and role-plays for kids*. California: Innerchoice Publishing.

Park, N., Peterson, C. & Seligman, M. (2004) 'Strengths of character and wellbeing.' *Journal of Social and Clinical Psychology*, Vol. 23, No. 5, 2004, pp. 603-619.

Peled, E., Jaffe, P. G. & Edleson, J. L. (1995) *Ending the Cycle of Violence: Community responses to battered women*. Thousand Oaks, CA: Sage Publications.

Peterson, C. & Park, N. (2003) 'Positive psychology as the even-handed positive psychology views it.' *Psychology Inquiry*, 14, 141-146.

Peterson, C. (2006) *A Primer in Positive Psychology*. Oxford: Oxford University Press.

Reivich, K. J., Gillham, J. E. & Shatte, A. (2004) *Penn Resiliency Program for Parents*. Unpublished.

Robinson, G. & Maines, B. (2008) *Bullying: A Complete Guide to the Support Group Method*. London: Sage Publications.

Rogers, C. R. (1942) *Counselling and Psychotherapy*. Boston: Houghton Mifflin.

Russell, B. (1951) *Impact of Science on Society*. New York: Columbia University Press.

Schoon, I. & Parsons, S. (2002) Competence in the face of adversity: the influence of early family environment and long-term consequences. *Children and Society*, 16, 260-272.

Seligman, M. (2003) *Authentic Happiness: Understanding the new positive psychology to realise your potential for lasting fulfillment*. London: Nicholas Brealey.

Seligman, M. E. P. & Csikszentimhayli, M. (2000) Positive Psychology: An introduction. *American Psychologist*, 55, 5-14.

Sharp, P. & Herrick, E. (2000) *Promoting Emotional Literacy: Anger management groups in clinical counselling in schools*, ed. Nick Barwick (2000). London: Routledge.

Snyder, C. R. & Lopez, S. (2002) *Handbook of Positive Psychology*. New York: Oxford University Press.

Sontag, S. (1989) *AIDS and its metaphors*. New York: Farrar, Straus & Giroux.

Spence, S. H., Donovan, C. & Brechman-Toussaint, M. (2000) 'The treatment of childhood social phobia: The effectiveness of a social skills training-based, cognitive-behavioural intervention, with and without parental involvement'. *Journal of Child Psychology and Psychiatry*, 41(6), 713-726.

Stott, D. (1974) *The Bristol Social Adjustment Guides: The Child in school and the child in the family. 5th Edition*. London: Hodder & Stoughton.

Sulzer-Azaroff, B. & Mayer, G. R. (1996) *Applying Behaviour-analysis Procedures with Children and Youth*. New York: Holt, Richards & Winston.

Werner, E. E. (1982) Vulnerable but Invincible: A longitudinal study of resilient children and youth: In Peterson, C. (2006) *A Primer In Positive Psychology*. Oxford: Oxford University Press.

White, R. W. (1959) Motivation re-considered: the concept of competence. *Psychological Review*, 66, 297-333.

Wilkin, A., Kinder, K., White, R., Atkinson, M. & Doherty, P. (2003) *Towards the Development of Extended Schools*. London: DfES.

Williams, B., Williams, J. & Ullman, A. (2002) Parental Involvement in Education. London: DfES (RR332).